Loving and Letting go

The Key to Being a Good Mom

Resources from MOPS

Books

Beyond Macaroni and Cheese
A Cure for the Growly Bugs and Other Tips for Moms
Getting Out of Your Kids' Faces and Into Their Hearts
Little Books for Busy Moms
  Time Out for Mom ... Ahhh Moments
  Great Books to Read and Fun Things to Do with Them
  If You Ever Needed Friends, It's Now
  Kids' Stuff and What to Do with It
Loving and Letting Go
Mom to Mom
Meditations for Mothers
A Mother's Footprints of Faith
Ready for Kindergarten
What Every Child Needs
What Every Mom Needs
When Husband and Wife Become Mom and Dad

Books with Drs. Henry Cloud and John Townsend

Raising Great Kids
Raising Great Kids for Parents of Preschoolers Workbook
Raising Great Kids for Parents of Teenagers Workbook
Raising Great Kids for Parents of School-Age Children Workbook

Gift Books

God's Words of Life from the Mom's Devotional Bible
Mommy, I Love You Just Because

Kids Books

Little Jesus, Little Me
My Busy, Busy Day
See the Country, See the City
Mommy, May I Hug the Fishes?
Mad Maddie Maxwell
Zachary's Zoo
Morning, Mr. Ted
Boxes, Boxes Everywhere
Snug as a Bug?

Bible

Mom's Devotional Bible

Audio

Raising Great Kids

Curriculum

Raising Great Kids for Parents of Preschoolers *Zondervan*Groupware™
(with Drs. Henry Cloud and John Townsend)

An Expanded and Updated Edition of
LEARNING TO LET GO

Loving and Letting go

The Key to Being a Good Mom

Foreword by Elisa Morgan
Carol Kuykendall

ZondervanPublishingHouse
Grand Rapids, Michigan

A Division of HarperCollinsPublishers

Loving and Letting Go
Copyright © 1985, 2000 by Carol Kuykendall

This book is an expanded and updated edition of *Learning to Let Go.*

Requests for information should be addressed to:

🏛ZondervanPublishingHouse
Grand Rapids, Michigan 49530

Library of Congress Cataloging-in-Publication Data

Kuykendall, Carol, 1945-
  Loving and letting go: the key to being a good mom / Carol Kuykendall.—Rev.
ed.
    p. cm.
  Rev. ed. of: Learning to let go. Grand Rapids, Mich.: Zondervan Pub. House,
c1985.
    ISBN: 0–310–23550–2 (softcover: alk. paper)
    1. Family—Religious life. 2. Parent and child 3. separation (Psychology) I.
Kuykendall, Carol, 1945- Learning to let go. II. Title
BV4526.2 .K88 2000
248.8'—dc 21   00–057218
                                                                                                              CIP

"Prayer for a Mother" by Evelyn Bence at the end of chapter 4 is from *Prayers for Girlfriends and Sisters and Me,* © 1999 by Evelyn Bence. Published by Servant Publications,
Box 8617, Ann Arbor, Michigan 48107. Used with permission.

"What a Mother Says" by Robin Gunn at the end of chapter 12 is from *Mothering by
Heart,* © 1996, by Robin Jones Gunn. Used by permission at Multnomah Publishers, Inc.

Interior design by Amy Langeler

Printed in the United States of America

00 01 02 03 04 05 /v DC/ 10 9 8 7 6 5 4 3 2

To all parents
who share this challenge of loving . . .
and letting go

Contents

Foreword 9

Acknowledgments 11

Introduction 13

1. Stirring Up the Nest 19
2. Head Knowledge and Heart Feelings 33
3. Control and Surrender 51
4. Overcoming Mommy Fears 65
5. Parental Patterns 79
6. Building a Firm Foundation 98
7. Early Training Rules 119
8. The Middle Years 134
9. Adolescence 150
10. Facing Transitions: "Get a Life, Mom!" 168
11. Fuzzy Release 184
12. Watching Them Soar 200

Epilogue 212

Notes 217

Foreword

I opened the door from the garage into the house to find a pile of clutter in my path. A doll cradle. Two dolls. A doll highchair. A mound of doll clothes. To the side, a doll house.

I had distinctly told Eva, then eleven, and Ethan, almost nine, to clean up the basement while I ran to the grocery store. What was this mess at the back door?

"Eva!" I called. "What's all this stuff?"

"Oh," she calmly responded, "that's to give away."

"Your dolls, and cradle, and highchair and dollhouse? Give away?" I asked in astonishment.

"Yeah. I don't need them anymore."

She didn't need them anymore. She didn't need them anymore?

This exchange about the issue of separation and forming an identity is only the most recent of many, many examples of my mothering days. From the time my children were tiny babies, I've been confronted with their intentions to separate from me and become people in their own right. Like the time both children literally pushed the bottle away from their lips and turned their head to resist it. They didn't need it anymore. And the moment when each decided to go away, far away to camp. For two weeks. Without me.

Externally, I have attempted to cheer such moments, convinced that they truly represent proof that my children are growing up well and that I am mothering the way I should. But internally, I've been a bit uncertain since they were babies. How much do I let go of my child and how soon?

In my work at MOPS International with thousands of mothers of preschoolers, I've heard many other moms ask the same questions. Carol Kuykendall's book answers them. Over the years we have recommended it time and time again, and moms of young children have cheered its message with letters and phone calls.

In her from-the-heart writing, Carol makes sense of a parent's ambivalence about the letting-go process. She mirrors our fears with stories of her own. Then she moves us to the point of understanding the health, and the importance, of this parental task. The goal of parenting is to mold a dependent infant into an independent adult. The process of creating an independent individual begins at birth, not at high school graduation.

Will we control, shield, and cocoon our children? Will we give in to the temptation to overlove, the instinct to overprotect? Such actions on our part could actually paralyze our children from reaching their potential.

When a son asks to cross the street alone, will we allow him to use the safety skills we've drilled into his head? When a toddler begs to "do it by myself!" will we withdraw our hands and accept the flour on the floor while she cookie cuts the dough? When an eleven-year-old announces she no longer needs her baby dolls, will we embrace her decision?

Letting go is a process that begins at birth and lasts for the lifetime of a child, and a parent. I'm just beginning to learn about this process. And how grateful I am that Carol can show me the way!

Elisa Morgan
President, MOPS International

Acknowledgments

The message of this book about loving and letting go lives within me today as passionately as it did when I first wrote about it, and I would like to thank the team at Zondervan Publishing House for giving me a second chance to research and revise the contents. Specifically, I'd like to thank Scott Bolinder, Sandy Vander Zicht, Brian Phipps, and Sue Brower. I'd also like to give a giant thank you to Evelyn Bence, the editor who rearranged some of the pieces, smoothed the transitions, and greatly helped to shape the final result.

To my friends at MOPS International, I extend thanks for their ongoing encouragement and guidance, especially Elisa Morgan, Mary Beth Lagerborg, and Karen Parks, who share not only a passion for the outreach of MOPS to every mom but also a love of books and writing. They have offered many contributions to this message.

Of course, I'd like to thank my family: my three children who have left the nest, Derek, Lindsay, and Kendall, for the ways they have continually helped me learn to let go and held me accountable for the lessons; and my husband, Lynn, for the many ways he encourages me and reminds me of all the good things still ahead in the next season of life.

Introduction

Before I became a mother, I imagined what mothering would be like.

Surely it would bring out the best in me. I'd take charge and be in complete control of my time, my emotions, and my children. I'd make the right decisions and then simply carry them out. I'd love my children well and let them go easily. Head over heart. Mind over matter. After all, that's what parents are supposed to do.

What was I thinking?

From the moment I became a mother, I began a process of transformation that is still changing who I am. Since the births of each of our three children, I've been filled with a growing, powerful mother love that affects the way I think and act. It both fills me to bursting and drains me to emptiness. It both confuses and consumes me. It brings out my best and my worst. It often tangles me up and keeps me from carrying out the right decision, even when I know what the right decision is. Mother love grips my heart and gets in the way of letting go, which is often the hardest part of parenting.

Yet the older I get, and the older my children get, the more I realize how God uses our children—as he uses all our life experiences—to teach us his most profound lessons, especially about this challenge of loving and letting go, which applies to all of life.

I wrote the first version of this book when our children were starting school and going on their first sleepovers, a time when I began to recognize this tugging conflict between my head and my heart. Their needs and endless questions and cuddly little bodies filled my days, so my descriptions about letting go in that season were fresh from my life as the mother of young children.

I'm revising it now from an empty nest where my husband, Lynn, and I live with our two dogs and my daughter's left-behind cat, which still meows mournfully for her. The children you will read about on these pages have grown up. Derek, twenty-eight, is married. Lindsay, twenty-six, is living and working in San Diego, and Kendall, twenty-three, is engaged. They live in various spots on the West Coast, far away from our home in Colorado, which is not how I expected life to be in this empty nest season. A long time ago, I made a bargain with God about that. I said, "It's fine, God, if these kids grow up and go away to school, but when it comes time for them to settle down—and especially when they start having children of their own, God—they need to come home. And home is where their mom lives."

So far they haven't come home, and as they get more and more settled down, I realize that home for them is probably not where their mom lives. Facing this reality reminds me that learning to let go is a lifelong challenge, a discovery that keeps my reflections focused and new as I tackle the revision of this book.

In each chapter, I am adding the perspective of my experiences as I look back over the years of raising children. The theme that runs throughout the book is this: loving comes easily, but letting go is difficult. Yet letting go is a critically important responsibility of parenting that meets a child's greatest need: to grow toward healthy independence. That is, after all, our goal as parents.

I believe this combination of voices—of a young mother's descriptions and an older mother's reflections—makes this book a unique offering about the loving and letting go that is necessary at every stage of mothering, especially the stage when our children are young. The patterns we form then usually set the tone for the way we live out this important responsibility. Do we choose dependence or independence? Do we overprotect our children, or encourage them to grow and go?

When children are toddlers, the questions are on one level— should I let him fall down when he's learning to walk, or should I always hold his hand? As children grow, the questions change, but they're borne out of the same instincts. Is he old enough to cross the street alone or ride a bike to a friend's house? Is she capable of buying her own clothes or determining who her friends should be? When do I give up my control and trust God to take over?

I was originally motivated to research this subject when I realized other parents were asking the same questions. "I read lots of books on how to bond with our children," a friend told me, "but none on how or when to cut some of those bonds."

I began gathering information from mothers, fathers, ministers, counselors, child psychologists, teachers, and authors. I asked them some key questions:

What does letting go mean?

Why is it difficult?

Why must we do it?

What does the Bible say?

How do we do it? And when?

As a result of my research, I found the most revealing answers came from parents like me who recognize that letting go is more than an intellectual choice or physical act. It is a complicated emotional challenge that tugs at our hearts and tests the foundations of our families.

In this new edition, you'll find plenty of time-tested tips, practical applications, updated resources, and some favorite quotes gathered over the years since I wrote the first version. At the end of each chapter, I've also added questions for personal reflection or discussion with a spouse—or for discussion with others, if you are reading with a group.

> "*Mothers are not meant for leaning upon. Mothers are meant to make leaning unnecessary.*"
>
> ❧

As you read, I trust you'll learn, as I have, that letting go means releasing our children and allowing them to become independent people. Years ago I read this quote: "Mothers are not meant for leaning upon. Mothers are meant to make leaning unnecessary."

As parents, we wrestle with this responsibility. It is a struggle—yes, a struggle—borne of good intentions and deep convictions. We love our children intensely. Instinctively we want to protect them and don't always recognize the ways we are holding on when we should be letting go.

This book seeks to help us recognize the difference. Admittedly, the information may not make letting go easier, but it may help us understand the importance of our responsibility to love our children—and to let them go.

PONDERPOINT

CONFESSIONS OF A MOM TRYING TO LET GO

"Here, son, put on this jacket."
"But I'm not cold."
"I am—so you *must* be."

"Honey, you could make the honor roll if you'd just try a little harder," I tell my daughter.
"I don't care, Mom," she responds with total indifference.
"You don't *care?* How could you not *care?*" I ask incredulously, because I *always* cared about

my grades, and suddenly I want to open up a vein in my arm and attach it to a vein in her arm and transfuse some of my passion directly into her.

My daughter comes home from the big dance in tears because she found out her date really likes someone else and only asked her on a dare from a friend.

As I comfort her, something inside me both boils and aches because her rejection opens up every rejection I've carried around in my heart since high school.

I look at my son's senior picture and I do not see an eighteen-year-old. I see a three-year-old.

Really, I do.

1

Stirring Up the Nest

> A neighbor said that our kids are like birds and
> when they learn to fly, we must let them go. So I did.
> But I have always left a little birdseed out and they
> fly back regularly. I am truly blessed.
>
> BEVERLY COOK, IN *A MOTHER'S TOUCH*

The early September day dawned cool and clear.

As I sat sipping my coffee at our kitchen counter, I thought about the meaning of this milestone morning. It was the first day of kindergarten, and Kendall, our youngest, had finally reached the magic age of five, which gave her the right to stuff her backpack full of her new school supplies and march out the door, down the driveway, and onto the school bus to begin a whole new adventure.

Suddenly she appeared in the kitchen, fully dressed and ready, a whole hour early.

"Is it time yet, Mom?" she asked, plopping down her backpack and climbing up on a stool next to me, acting like some suddenly grown-up person.

Obviously she was excited, while I was torn between a bitter-sweet twinge of joy and regret.

I had thought I was looking forward to this day just as she was. After all, I had been home with little children for the last eleven years. In spite of periodic temptations to give up full-time mothering and seek the imagined fulfillment of a nine-to-five job, I chose to work part-time at home and arrange my days around peanut butter and jelly sandwiches, naptime schedules, and hectic preschool carpools.

Symbolically this September day would mark the beginning of the freedom I'd anticipated for years: freedom to pursue dreams I'd postponed; freedom to develop neglected friendships; freedom to explore the possibilities of the next season of life. Instead of excitement, however, I felt sadness at the finality this moment represented. Even as I poured cereal into a bowl for Kendall, I realized this day also marked the end of a stage of mothering. When Kendall stepped on that bus this morning, she would be stepping into a new world of her own, and I was stepping back, to take on a permanent, more part-time status in the lives of my children.

> *I hugged her and held her tightly ... and then let her go.*

The planned obsolescence of mothering, I thought as I looked at my girl-baby perched on this kitchen stool, taking her treasures out of her backpack with her chubby preschool hands. I grabbed the camera and caught the moment.

"Oh, Kendall, I don't want you to grow up and go off to school. How about if you stay home with me forever?"

"Oh brother, Mom," she said, rolling her eyes.

An hour later, I tried to swallow my nostalgia and share Kendall's joy as I walked her down the driveway, camera in hand again. As the big yellow bus lumbered to a stop at our gate, I hugged her and held her tightly ... and then let her go.

Tears stung my eyes. I snapped a picture of her as the bus swallowed her up. I couldn't even find her in the windows full of laughing faces when the bus pulled away, marking the beginning of a time when the boundaries in her life would be out of my sight.

I turned and walked down the long driveway to our house.

Inside, I poured another cup of coffee. *Why should this normal anticipated event cause me to feel sad?* I asked myself and wandered aimlessly around a strangely quiet and empty house. *After all, this independence is what I want for my child.*

I got out my Bible, sank down in a chair by the window, and blew a ripple over the surface of the steaming coffee. Gazing out the window, I noticed a beautiful large bird gracefully soaring over the field. Tawny with distinctive white markings, it had a powerful wide wingspan.

Mommy Birds

Mommy birds have the right idea, I decided. They feed and care for their baby birds, and then one day, when it's time, they merely nudge them out of the nest with no regrets, because that's the thing to do. They don't get all tangled up with concerns about the big scary world of predators out there. They don't get self-absorbed with sadness about living in an empty nest. They push the babies out of the nest, off they fly, and the mommies get on with life. Period. Done. Finished.

Here I was, zooming ahead and imagining life in the empty nest, which sounded so dreadfully bleak—and empty. Just a few days before, a friend had stopped by after sending the last of her five children to college. "It's awful," she admitted, trying to laugh in spite of the quiver in her voice. "After twenty-six years of having kids around, suddenly the house is too big and lonely. We can't remember where the years went."

I continued to watch the large bird in the bright blue sky. I was so captivated by its circling and soaring that I didn't even notice the smaller bird with identical markings, now darting in quick jerky movements around the larger bird.

I soon realized this was a baby bird testing its wings while the larger bird circled and followed, swooping underneath and circling again. Following, leaving, returning, circling, and following again, the graceful larger bird tirelessly continued its watchful pattern. For these two birds, this moment was nothing more than a normal training session. For me it was a revelation about letting go. Birds may nudge their young out of the nest, but they are not done with their young after the nudging. The revelation reminded me of what I've learned about eagles teaching their eaglets to fly. There's a passage in the Bible that describes this process: ". . . like an eagle that stirs up its nest and hovers over its young, that spreads its wings to catch them and carries them on its pinions" (Deut. 32:11).

Letting go is a two-part process for the eagle mothers. First they "stir up" the nest, making it less comfortable by removing layers of soft materials to reveal sharp prickly twigs that encourage the eaglet to test its wings. Author Ron Hutchcraft notes that the mother eagle "realizes her babies need a little help venturing out of the nest. So when the eaglets are getting old enough to learn to fly, Mother Eagle starts to 'uncomfort' the nest. She starts to put sharp sticks and stones inside so Baby Eagle will be motivated to get out and soar."[1] This stirring up and nudging is actually an act of love, because what good is an eagle that can't fly?

Then the parent eagle begins a time of training, standing by during those test flights, fluttering over its young, spreading out its wings, catching the eaglet when it falls, patiently correcting, teaching, and encouraging it to try again. Finally, when the eaglet is capable, it flies away, strong and free and alone, ready and able to seek its potential in life because of the training it received. Describing the majestic bird's transition, Hutchcraft writes, "Mother Eagle's lesson? 'If your kids are ever going to fly, you need to be an ally of their freedom.' Unfortunately, many children get the impression that they have to fight their mother and father to get out of the nest!"

Soon the birds outside my window circled and disappeared. Together. At that moment I knew their appearance was more than a coincidence. It was God's comforting reminder that he has a purpose in our loving and letting go, which is carried out in all of his creation. It is not a single one-time event but an ongoing orderly process of encouragement and training, and just like the mother eagle, my part in the process helps my children become all he created them to be.

While we have our children in the nest, our responsibility is to both nurture and nudge. As we squeeze all the joy and love and training out of our precious years together, we must also stir up the nest, encouraging our children to test their wings at the appropriate moments, like the first day of school. Although the nudging may not feel as good as the nurturing, it is a vital part of the plan for their lives and ours. Unless they go, they can't reach their potential. Unless we let them go, we aren't free to see what God has in store for us in a later season of life.

I thanked God for these reflections at a moment when I most needed them, but in the next few days and years, I still wrestled with questions and challenges.

LETTING GO: IS IT WORTH IT?

A friend, a newlywed at the time, said something that surprised me one day. We were sitting at a picnic table in a park near her office, eating a quick lunch while my two young children played on the swings nearby. She told me she didn't think she and her husband would have children. "You invest yourself so deeply and emotionally; you worry about them all the time, wondering whether you're doing a good job and whether they'll turn out, and then in a few short years, they're gone! It just seems like a bunch of headaches and heartaches," she said. "So maybe I'll just borrow yours when I need a kid fix!"

For a moment I didn't know how to respond. Partly because I couldn't imagine life without my two children—ages three and five—and partly because I was distracted by watching them and worrying about their safety.

"Careful, Lindsay!" I yelled when I saw her trying to climb off her moving swing. Derek, the "older brother," quickly came to her aid, and in a sudden display of tender, protective sibling love, he stopped her swing and helped her off. How could I ever describe to my friend what it's like to witness a moment like that between your own children?

How do you explain that having children is worth the pain of childbirth, the sleepless nights, the emotional cost of love and loss—though I knew little about loss at that time in my life? That it's worth all the worries, trips to the emergency room, fears about their future? All that in exchange for sticky kisses, a refrigerator door covered with smudgy pictures of pointy suns and uneven rainbows, and declarations that "you are the best mom in the whole world."

How could I tell her that investing yourself is worth it? How could I tell her this, since she was childless and living a romantic uncomplicated life (except for her dog) and had probably read that infamous Ann Landers column that stated some 70 percent of the parents responding to a survey said they wouldn't have kids if they could start over again?

Then I thought about our first dog, who was also our "first child" when we were newlyweds. Pets often provide a valuable preview for young married couples. So I told her about Rhody, our golden retriever from Rhode Island, where we lived while Lynn was in the navy. I raised her from a pup—newspaper training, obedience classes, the whole routine. She was a good dog, but she had her faults. She loved to play "escape," especially when I was on my way out of the house for work or an appointment. So over the years, I spent plenty of hours worrying about her and frantically searching the neighborhood for her.

She cost us a lot not only in vet bills and kennel charges but also in rental payments. Apartments would have been fine for us, but we always looked for small houses or duplexes with yards so Rhody would have a place to play. We often gave up spur-of-the-moment trips or dinner after work because we had to get home to let the dog in or out. She needed exercise and would drop her soggy tennis ball at our feet for hours on end, begging for a game of fetch.

But I bonded with that dog for thirteen years, and when we finally buried her in the field behind our house, I cried and grieved our loss. She had enriched our days, widened our circle of love, and taught us some valuable lessons on life. I missed her romping around the house, and yet I'm forever grateful she was part of our family.

I wasn't sure my friend understood what I was saying that day, but three years later she was a happy (and tired) new mom. Yes, as she had previously guessed, loving and letting go is not easy. It's downright painful. For most of us, the deeper we invest ourselves in the lives of our children, the greater the pain. The more we wrap our lives around them, the harder it is to unwrap ourselves.

It doesn't seem fair. But God rejects worldly notions of fairness. In God's economy, everything seems to work backward. The Bible tells us that the last shall be first. We're here to serve, not to be served. We receive when we give, and we give without expectation of reward or return. Also, love costs, and pain is often the price we pay for sacrificing ourselves and doing what is best for those we love, even when that isn't always what feels best for us. After all, mothering is not all about us. It's about doing what is best for our children.

LETTING GO: WHY IS IT SO HARD?

We raise our children to leave us. We know that's the way it should be. Why, then, does letting go feel so difficult at times? Why do we get all tangled up in the process and hold on when we should let go? Why is it so hard?

> *Why do we get all tangled up in the process and hold on when we should let go?*

I've struggled with these questions for years and discovered several answers.

First, the holding-on instinct is so powerful. Let's start at the very beginning, when we—if we are birth mothers—carried that child under our hearts for nine months. Our baby's kick was our pain but also our precious reminder of the miracle growing within us. Lovingly we waited for the first glimpse and touch of this baby we already intimately knew.

In his book *Bonding,* Dr. Donald Joy describes the typical birthing instinct:

> Mothers are "encompassers." Even during delivery, the mother instinctively reaches out to receive and hold the baby to herself. . . .
>
> The literal umbilical attachment tends to continue in a psychological attachment; mothering is borderline connectedness throughout life. In the early years the child imagines itself to be an extension of the mother. It ventures out from the mother as "center" and runs back to her as "safety."[2]

A baby's utter dependence on and attachment to us—the nursing lips, the grip of a finger, the first smile—draw out the protective nesting instincts that are critically important in those early days, months, and years. In this stage of their lives, love is nearly synonymous with protection, with physical closeness, with constant care.

And yet things change.

Our instincts, which help sustain an infant's life, must evolve as that child grows, and it's a simple fact that change is hard. Even positive change. I remember the bittersweet feeling of weaning each of our three children, a preview to me of all the little and big unattachings that lay ahead. I remember the first time my daughter's friend took the place of me—the mom—as her number-one confidante. Normal, healthy—but hard—changes.

As our children grow up, our love may not change in intensity, but the way we express that love must change, as will the way they show their love for us. Slowly as they mature, we must give up control and protection so they learn to control and protect themselves.

Letting go is also difficult because the day-to-day issues and reality fill us with ambivalence. We love our children, yet they can irritate us, and in our weakest moments, when the noise level in the house is high and the satisfaction level is low, we long for the quiet days of a house with no children. Yet that very evening—when the children are all snuggled in their beds, smelling good and looking cherubic—we can't imagine life without them; we like things just the way they are, right here and now, and want to freeze them forever at this stage. The ambivalence inherent in any close familial relationship confuses us. The confusion can make us wonder if we're doing it all wrong.

I think life must be simpler for a mother eagle, don't you?

Actually, for me, letting go is a continuing challenge because I am an instinctive nurturer and nest-maker. I love each of our three children and would do almost anything for them, which means I sometimes lose my perspective and do too much for them, smothering them in the name of love instead of urging them to test their wings. I have been known to do all the wrong things for all the right reasons. Why? Because I love them.

I have held on when I should have let go, because their going stings, especially when I became aware of some subtle little sign that reminded me they were growing up and away: the day I realized I had permanently become Mom instead of Mommy; the time I discovered a DO NOT DISTURB sign on the door of the bedroom where I'd always been welcome; the first time my child refused his usual goodbye kiss because his friends might see; the day I heard, "Please don't wear *that* skirt to Field Day, Mom," or, "Just wait in the car when you come pick me up." Once upon a time, I could do no wrong in their eyes. I could burn the toast, choose their clothes, even tell the barber how to cut their hair, without any criticism from them; eventually I couldn't even choose my own clothes without their comments.

More signs are evident when children become teens: the first family vacation without the child who chooses to stay home; the first Thanksgiving with an empty place at the table; and the disappearance of the DO NOT DISTURB signs on bedroom doors because the occupants are gone. All these are perfectly predictable, even desirable, steps toward independence, but they feel painful because each removes some of the soft comforting layers in our cozy nest and reveals another twig.

Our challenge as parents is to view these steps of independence with joy instead of regret, for they tell us we are doing our job as parents. When Kendall climbed on that school bus with enthusiasm and confidence on her first day of kindergarten, she didn't linger or look back. She was testing her wings, and naturally I felt a twinge of regret, wishing I could share the very same airspace she claimed as her own. But her confidence told me I was succeeding in the challenge God had given me.

As our children pass each milestone of independence, they remind us we are reaching the goal of our parenting, which is to raise children who are capable of coping in the world without us at their sides all the time; children who learn to depend on God, not us.

Of course, letting go is not always easy. God doesn't promise that his challenges will be easy. Nothing worthwhile is ever accomplished without a measure of sacrifice. But he promises us his presence; he promises that these changes bring necessary growth for us and for our children. As I look back on those days following Kendall's departure for kindergarten, I see how quickly I adjusted and discovered a new burst of energy to tackle projects I'd put off for years.

GUIDELINES OF LOVING AND LETTING GO

Letting go is a lifelong challenge for parents. As the birds reminded me that day, letting go is not a single event. It doesn't happen all at once on the day a child gets on a school bus or leaves home for college, marriage, or a job in another city. Rather it is a slow, physical and emotional process that begins the moment the umbilical cord is cut at birth. It continues in little steps and starts, moment by moment, as a child grows up. It is, in fact, a process with specific goals, characteristics, and a logical order. The process slowly prepares the child for independence. But that's not all; it also prepares the parents for life without the child, for a new season filled with its own joys and challenges.

Before we delve deeper into issues of loving and letting go, here are some guidelines which are foundational to the rest of the book. As you finish later chapters, you might want to turn back to this page to review the basics. Even after you've finished the book, these guidelines will help you bring perspective to the process of loving and letting go.

1. Letting go is one of the most critical responsibilities of parenting that meets a child's greatest need: to grow toward healthy independence.
2. Letting go is a lifelong process that starts the moment the umbilical cord is cut at birth and continues in little steps and starts, moment by moment, as a child grows up.

3. Letting go demands a gradual change in the way we express our love for our children, from total control in infancy to no control in maturity. The goal is to take care of them until they can take care of themselves.

4. Letting go is a process marked by the balanced orderly granting of appropriate freedom and responsibility, year by year, as the child grows up.

5. Letting go means we encourage and reward (not thwart) appropriate steps of independence. Their success is our success.

6. Letting go recognizes that we raise our children to leave us. Throughout this process, we (1) equip our children for life beyond our homes and (2) prepare ourselves for life when they are no longer in our homes. Our goal is to work ourselves out of the parenting job and reach an adult-to-adult relationship with our children.

There's an old saying about giving your children both roots and wings. Yes, children need roots that anchor them deeply. But when I think about the process in terms of birds, especially of soaring eagles. I say give your children nests and wings.

Warm cozy nests stabilize little ones and protect them against dangerous assaults. Nests are safe and secure woven together with bonds of love. They are places to spend time together in close quarters, making memories and observing traditions. Nests provide a nurturing world.

Wings lift children upward and give them hope. Wings grow stronger with our stirring up the nest. Wings grow stronger with test flights, while we're still close by to encourage them. Strong wings allow them to soar freely and close to God.

Children need both—nests and wings.

Cozy nests I can handle; strong wings are my challenge.

FOR REFLECTION

1. Think of a recent example of your child's need for independence. What was your response?

2. What aspect of letting go is most difficult for you?

3. Which is a greater challenge for you: making nests or strengthening wings? Which was a greater challenge for your mother? What similarities and differences do you see?

4. Think in terms of nests and wings or nurturing and nudging. Identify ways you have provided or encouraged both for your child in the last week.

5. What would you like to learn about letting go as you read this book?

PONDERPOINT

A PRAYER FOR OUR CHILDREN

I pray they will know Jesus.

I pray they will learn to love others with kindness and compassion.

I pray they will know the difference between right and wrong and will pursue what is right.

I pray they will develop self-control and self-discipline.

I pray they will respect those in authority.

I pray they will desire the right kind of friends.

I pray they will resist temptation and hold fast to the truth.

I pray they will find joy in the right mate and
be saved in purity for that person.
I pray they will be filled with God's hope.

CAROL KUYKENDALL

2

Head Knowledge and Heart Feelings

The parenting books ... give the impression that the
right consistent formula will win out every time.

ELIZABETH CODY NEWENHUYSE,
SOMETIMES I FEEL LIKE RUNNING AWAY FROM HOME

In my first few years of mothering, I became a parenting-expert junkie. I read the books and listened to the tapes. My husband and I attended parenting classes and talks at church or almost anywhere else within a fifty-mile radius of our home. I watched TV talk shows and listened to radio programs and sought advice from other parents I admired.

I collected a headful of knowledge, assuming this would guarantee I'd be a good mother who made good decisions. But here's the surprise: sometimes all that head knowledge disappeared in an instant because something more powerful took over.

My heart feelings.

Here's a typical example.

Late one afternoon while grocery shopping with both a toddler and a preschooler stuffed into my cart (the same two children who had been pushing me to my limits all day long), I totally lost my ability to think rationally. They were whining about being hungry. I was hungry. We were all tired. They wanted cookies. I have to admit, I wanted cookies too. More than cookies, I wanted peace. No whining.

"Please, Mommy, please, Mommy. Mommy! Cookies. We want cookies."

Everything in my head told me, *You don't give children cookies just because they whine for cookies. You don't give children cookies an hour before dinner. Saying no to cookies builds character in children and teaches them about delayed gratification and reinforces the fact that you—the mother—are the one in control here.*

"Please, Mommy. I need a cookie! Cookie!" they said in unison, pointing to a package on the shelf in the long cookie aisle.

Something inside me snapped. I don't know exactly what. But I do remember grabbing the package off the shelf, ripping it open, and then handing cookies to the two children in my cart. I think I even ate a couple myself.

It didn't make sense, but it made silence, and at that moment I wanted silence more than sense, even though the decision went against everything I knew.

Later I felt guilty when the checker lifted the half-empty package of cookies out of my cart.

"It's okay," she said with a grin. "I'm a mom too."

For a moment she and I shared an intimate understanding of how our heart feelings sometimes win out over our head knowledge.

As parents we know many things about loving and about letting go. But for any number of reasons—compassion, fatigue, impatience, insecurity, or plain old desire to please our kids—we sometimes ignore our head knowledge and give in to our heart feelings. Before we look at more of those heart feelings, let's get a firm grasp on the head knowledge that underlies the letting-go process. What is loving and letting go, and why is it so important?

LETTING GO IS ...

Letting go is a broad concept, key to coping with life's everyday challenges. Generally it means choosing to relinquish something—a treasure of the heart, a difficult memory, a grudge, pride, an unfulfilled dream—to receive something more important or better. A short-term loss for a long-range greater good. It often requires head over heart, mind over matter, faith over fear. If we are letting go of something, we must recognize our conflicted feelings but choose to put them aside or rise above them or do something in spite of them. Letting go is an important concept in all of life, not just with our parenting. Let me give you an example.

> *Letting go means choosing to relinquish something to receive something more important or better. A short-term loss for a long-range greater good.*

For years while our children were young, we lived next door to my mother, who had emphysema, the result of scar tissue that formed in her lungs when she was a child. My father had already passed away, and she lived alone. We built a house on land adjacent to hers so I could help care for her and so our children could run across the field on a well-worn path to see her. This was a delight of her life—and theirs too. In the final stages of the disease, she also had a woman named Dessie living downstairs who could help her in the night if necessary.

Dessie called me early one August morning.

"Your mother thinks she's having a heart attack," she said. "She needs you."

I raced across the field, into the house, and to her bedside.

"It's okay, Mother," I said, taking her hand and trying to control the panic rising in my chest. "Relax and breathe gently, just like me," I pleaded. I put my face close to hers and tried to talk her out of dying.

She shook her head slightly. "This is just the way I wanted it," she whispered, referring to her wish to die quickly when the moment came. For years she had suffered, and she feared a slow suffocating death from the relentless disease.

She held my hand and relaxed, and a few moments later, it was all over. My sixty-seven-year-old mother was gone.

For weeks after that, I couldn't shake the vivid memory of watching her die and of feeling so helpless. To come to terms with my mother's death—to let go of her and of the death scene itself—I had to make a prayerful and intentional effort to let go of that haunting memory so I could replace it with the joyful ones of her healthier days and the victory she achieved in dying.

Choosing to let go can usher us into a freer, more contented place. A woman lets go of her rigid expectations of marriage to live with and learn to love her husband of ten years. A mother lets go of her fanatical desire for a spotless house to allow her children to make cookies, have friends over, or experiment with projects for the science fair. A dad, the neighborhood soccer coach, has to let go of his desire to win the big game (which he could win with his star players) to rotate all of the players in and out of the lineup fairly. A person has to let go of anger and resentment to make room for forgiveness, to let go of fears about tomorrow to experience the joys of today.

Letting go is key to living out our faith and our lives. Letting go is also key to reaching our parenting goals. Here are some of the reasons why letting go of our children is important.

WE LET GO BECAUSE . . .

WE LET GO BECAUSE WE LOVE THEM

The first compelling reason we must let go is because we love our children and want what is best for them. Consider for a moment our hopes. What do we want out of life for them? What qualities do we hope they possess when they leave home?

When these questions were posed to a Christian parenting group recently, they quickly came up with these answers, in no particular order:

- Personal relationship with Christ
- Desire for spiritual growth
- Good character
- Development of self-esteem and confidence
- Ability to withstand peer pressure
- Knowledge of their gifts and strengths
- Appreciation for the value of family
- Ability to accept responsibility
- Ability to make good choices

If we look over these goals, we know the route to reaching them is through our children's gradual release from us as parents. We want them to have a personal relationship with Christ, but they don't inherit that from us. They must choose that for themselves.

We hope they will make good choices in life, recognize their strengths, and gain a sense of responsibility and perseverance, but those qualities come from learning to pick themselves up after failing, especially when we're not around to help. We have to give them the freedom to gain confidence in themselves apart from us. We have to let go.

"One of the highest priorities I have is to teach my children to live life without me," author Karen Burton Mains told a roomful of mothers at a women's conference. "I want them to learn to be dependent on their heavenly Father, who will always be with them—I won't."

WE LET GO BECAUSE THE TIES THAT BIND CAN ALSO STRANGLE

Because we love our children, we can unwittingly stunt their growth toward independence with our overprotection. It's easy to do because providing protection is a characteristic of a love relationship.

One afternoon a few years ago, I visited my seventy-four-year-old father-in-law in the hospital. He was recovering from minor surgery, but the experience frightened him, and he shared his concern that he had not prepared my mother-in-law for life without him.

"I think I've done too much for her over the years," he said regretfully. "Driving her places, paying the bills, fixing everything. Now I'm worried she can't get along on her own."

> *We have a responsibility not to allow our protective love to stifle their growth.*

When we love someone, we enjoy doing things for that person, but we also have a responsibility not to allow our protective love to stifle their growth—especially our children. We have to realize that we can hurt them by doing too much.

Dr. James Dobson recognizes our instinctive protective love but encourages parents to temper it:

We want to rise like a mighty shield to protect them from life's sting—to hold them snugly within the safety of our embrace. Yet there are times when we must let them struggle. Children can't grow without taking risks. Toddlers can't walk initially without falling down. Students can't learn without facing some hardships. And ultimately, an adolescent can't enter young adulthood until we release him from our protective custody.[1]

WE LET GO BECAUSE WE CANNOT CONTROL THEIR LIVES

Though we are in control of many of the circumstances affecting our younger children, we quickly learn that ultimately we cannot control their lives, especially as they get older. A father told me how he's learned to let go in situations where he has no control. "We've faced a lot of crises in high school and college with our four kids. Drugs, school failures, eating problems, lack of motivation," he said. "The pivotal point in each crisis was letting go. We told them we couldn't control their behavior, so the responsibility and therefore the consequences were theirs. We continued to offer support and advice, but we intentionally stepped back. Sometimes that meant exercising tough love. In each case, there was a dramatic change. They had to take control and solve the problems."

WE LET GO IN OBEDIENCE TO GOD

Letting go fulfills God's plan for families, which is described in the biblical directive that gave us independence when we got married: "A man will leave his father and mother and be united to his wife, and they will become one flesh" (Gen. 2:24). Our letting go prepares our children to grow up and separate from us and become husbands and wives and parents of their own families someday.

The apostle Paul uses a familial image to represent spiritual growing up. To immature Christians he writes, "I gave you milk, not solid food, for you were not yet ready for it" (1 Cor. 3:2), implying that a healthy mature person thrives on solid food, not baby food. Paul also gives insight into how one grows into adulthood: "When I was a child, I talked like a child, I thought like a child, I reasoned like a child. When I became a man, I put childish ways behind me" (1 Cor. 13:11).

Our children will not give up their childish ways as long as they are dependent on us. They cannot grow to full healthful maturity unless we withdraw our control from their lives and allow them age-appropriate independence. We have to give them the freedom to grow and go and fulfill God's purpose for their lives.

But Jesus said we should become like children to enter God's kingdom (Mark 10:15). Does that contradict Paul's exhortation to put away childish things? There's a world of difference between being childlike (spontaneous, receptive, trusting, full of wonder) and being childish. Jesus himself gives us an example of a child growing up and going away to fulfill his heavenly Father's purpose.

The Bible tells us God has a plan for our children, just as he has a plan for each one of us: to draw them to himself. To give them a future and a hope. To complete the good work he has begun in them. Our children are first and foremost his, and we must let go to allow God to guide them toward the discovery of his plan for them.

WE LET GO FOR OUR OWN GOOD

Our children's growing independence is not only good for them but also good for us. During the child-rearing season of life, we expect certain things. We expect, for instance, to put forth a maximum amount of time and energy during our children's infancy and toddler years. We expect to get a bit of a break during their school years, not only because they are away from home more often but also because they can do more for themselves and make more of their own decisions. If we do not allow this change to occur naturally, we are likely to get tired. I like the poem by Nancy McConnell that compares motherhood to teaching a child to ride a bike:

> Being a mother is
> a lot like teaching a child
> to ride a bicycle.

You have to know when
to hold on and when to
let go. If you lack this courage
to let go, you'll get very tired of running along
beside.[2]

This parental fatigue has been called "parent burnout." Joseph Procaccini, a national authority on family relationships and author of a book on the subject, describes burnout as a physically, emotionally, and sometimes spiritually exhausted reaction to the stress of raising children. He estimates burnout affects about half of the parents in the United States, both fathers and mothers. According to Procaccini, parents especially vulnerable to burnout are those who want to control children even through adulthood. These parents have the script, and they are the directors; children are to perform accordingly. This is in contrast to parents who are developers—people who provide the basic support for a child's growth and progress but are willing to change with the child.[3]

WE LET GO FOR THEIR OWN GOOD

If we think about it, we know that the consequences of not letting go are frightening: children never experiencing separation from parents in a church nursery or at home with a baby-sitter; children never learning to cross the street alone, never making purchases and getting the right change at the store, never learning to make good choices on their own. In later chapters we'll look at specifics about parenting children at various ages. But here we're simply identifying some signs of paralyzing overprotection, which involves inappropriate attempts to control a child's environment.

Our children's preschool teacher used the term "smother mothers" for moms who lingered longer than necessary at school each morning, hanging up her child's coat, tying on the paint apron, helping to spread peanut butter on a cracker, and doing all the other things the child is capable of doing.

"Not only is this unhealthy for the mother," the teacher said, "but it robs the child of the important sense of self-confidence he or she needs to be building at this stage of life."

"Helicopter mothers" is another term for mothers who hover over their children, waiting to rescue a child from any distressing situation. Hovering also is a form of overprotection.

My daughter had a friend whose mother always had an excuse why her nine-year-old couldn't go swimming with us, sleep over at our house, or go to a movie. This child rarely went anywhere without her parents. This same mother couldn't understand why her daughter was afraid to start school at the beginning of fourth grade.

CONSEQUENCES OF OVERPROTECTION

As a mother, I know in my head that there are consequences of overprotecting my children.

Overprotection can easily thwart our ultimate parenting goals. We run the risk of raising emotionally handicapped children who are confined by dependence on their parents. They lack the confidence to try a new experience, make a decision, or face life alone. They may be twenty-three and still living at home trying to find themselves while Mom and Dad are footing the bills, getting their meals, and doing the laundry.

But not all children comply with overprotection. Some dramatically rebel to defy their parents and finally free themselves of their parents' stifling control. Anorexia, bulimia, and other eating disorders sometimes result from overprotection.

Running away from home is another form of rebellion. One sixteen-year-old girl, the only child of overly protective parents who insisted on driving her to and from high school each day, suddenly disappeared. Though she had always appeared compliant, she ran away to the streets of New York City with little money and no friends in order to free herself from her parents' smothering protection. Eventually she returned home to parents who finally realized they had to give her more independence and allow her to think for herself.[4]

A study of runaways and their relationships with their parents identifies three ways parents delay or prevent a child's separation while actually triggering that child's decision to rebel.

Affective binding is characterized by the parent overindulging the child with rewards. "Giving, in this sense, has less to do with the real needs of the child than the parental drive to maintain strong, manipulative control over the child and thus prevent the child from becoming autonomous."

Cognitive binding happens when parents impose their perceptions and definitions upon their children to prevent them from acknowledging their own feelings or learning to think for themselves. This results in low self-esteem and gets children into the habit of listening to voices outside of their heads instead of inside. This in turn makes them more susceptible to peer pressure and being led by others who are stronger than themselves, because they are accustomed to being told what to do.

Superego binding is parents' exploitation of their children's loyalties. Children are made to feel guilty at any thought of reducing their loyalties to their parents.

All three types of parental behavior work toward the same result: keeping the children unnaturally close to the parents.[5]

Many parents assume their protection communicates love and value to the child. They assume the child is receiving the message that "you mean so much to me that I am taking extra special good care of you." Instead the opposite is true, especially with overprotection. The child actually receives the message that "you are not capable of taking care of yourself." As one child told his mom, "Every time you help me like that, you make me feel helpless." The parents' attempts to express their love through overprotection result in the child's lack of confidence and low self-esteem. Overprotecting our children puts us in a place of permanent parenthood and puts them into permanent childhood. Instead of overprotection, we need to give them the freedom to make choices—and the freedom to fail.

LETTING GO: FREEDOM FOUNDATIONS

Let's look at three principles for letting go and gradually giving children age-appropriate freedoms.

FREEDOM TO MAKE CHOICES AND ACCEPT THE CONSEQUENCES

So much of life involves making choices: What shall I wear? Which class should I choose? Which task will I tackle first? Which job should I take? In an effort to build confidence in their ability to make choices, we begin allowing children to make simple choices with lesser consequences when they are young. As they grow, our role becomes advisory. We give fewer commands and more information. We help them look at their options and consider the pros and cons of each. Our goal is to teach them how to think, not what to think. And the more we allow them to think for themselves, the more they care about what we think. They learn we won't force them to think what we think. We listen to their opinions and ideas and, when appropriate, let them make choices for themselves.

As they get older, we have to understand that even giving our opinions in some instances may make their decisions more difficult. "Please don't tell me what you think, Mom," fourteen-year-old Derek pleaded with me one day. "I have a hard time separating it from what I think."

Several years later, when Derek was a college freshman and had gained more confidence in making his own decisions, he called home long distance for some advice. "I'd like your opinion about whether I should continue to play on the basketball team," he told us, "but I want you to know that in the end, I'm going to make up my own mind, and you may not agree with my decision." Because the decision did not affect us financially, he was right in owning the decision and the consequences. By the time our children leave home, our role is to offer opinions when asked and to accept their decisions.

FREEDOM TO FAIL

Tempting as it is, we should not protect our children from failure. Their lives, like ours, are shaped more by failure than by success. "Consider it pure joy, my brothers, whenever you face trials of many kinds, because you know that the testing of your faith develops perseverance" (James 1:2–3). Trials and suffering strengthen the soul. If we stand by our children with love and support, they will learn from their failures, even as the Prodigal Son did. The boy took his inheritance and left home. His father knew he couldn't cope with that much money and that much freedom. Sure enough, the boy squandered his money in loose living and soon was penniless and hungry. How much his father must have wanted to help his son out. But he didn't. As a result, the son learned from his experience and returned home to ask his father's forgiveness.

"Please give me the freedom to make decisions concerning myself. Permit me to fail, so that I can learn from my mistakes. Then someday I'll be prepared to make the kind of decisions life requires of me," writes Dr. Kevin Leman in "Child's Ten Commandments to Parents."[6]

FREEDOM TO ASSUME THEIR OWN RESPONSIBILITIES

Because we love our children, we too often assume responsibilities that are rightfully theirs. Here's a typical example from the early morning rush hour at our house when our children were in elementary school.

The digital clock on the stove read out the minutes until "blastoff time," which was 8:06, the time the school bus arrived at the end of our driveway. The kids were wolfing down their cereal; the dog was barking to be fed; there was the frenzied last-minute search for books, homework papers, jump ropes, and the polished rock for show and tell. Suddenly it was time, and with one final flurry, the kids raced out the door. A few minutes later, as I swept up the crumbs, I discovered that one child had left the homework paper she had worked so hard to do the night before.

The presence of that piece of paper on the counter set off a major conflict between my head and heart; it presented a major challenge to letting go. What should I do about it? Deliver it to school for her ... or not?

In my head, I knew I should leave that homework paper right on the counter. That's the right answer. But I have to confess. Sometimes something more powerful takes over.

It was my heart feelings ... again.

Sometimes I got in the car and beat the bus to school and met her with the paper as she went in the school door. And the look of relief and gratitude on her face made my heart sing. Sure, I admit that I liked to be Mighty Mother and rescue her from pain. But more than that, I hoped she would see a glimpse of God's grace in that gesture of kindness, a glimpse that would encourage her to treat others with the same kindness. Not because any of us deserves that treatment, but because we are loved.

In her book *Traits of a Healthy Family*, Dolores Curran encourages parents to allow their children to assume responsibilities, because irresponsible children grow into irresponsible adults. Healthy families "tend to insist that members take full responsibility for their actions, and doing that means living with the consequences of irresponsibility," she writes. "Our real responsibility as parents is to offer them the opportunity to grow in responsibility, not assume their responsibilities because they are our children."[7] That's the right answer, most of the time.

Dr. Henry Cloud and Dr. John Townsend call this the balance between truth and grace, which is necessary for a child to grow. Here's their formula:

> Give a person grace (unmerited favor) and truth (structure) and do that over time, and you have the greatest chance of this person growing into a person of good character.

Grace includes support, resources, love, compassion, forgiveness, and all of the relational sides of God's nature. Truth is the structure of life; it tells us how we are supposed to live our lives and how life really works.[8]

Finding the balance is our challenge as parents.

CONFLICTS OF HEAD AND HEART

Knowing how to find that balance between truth and grace, or head and heart, is not always as clear as the experts make it sound in their books. As Elizabeth Cody Newenhuyse notes, "The parenting books assume that the world of children is rational and well ordered. . . . They give the impression that the right consistent formula will win out every time."[9]

We face a challenge to balance head knowledge with heart feelings and make choices that will lead to the best and most loving results in the long run. In the midst of our dilemmas and distractions, we often have to go back to basics.

That's a lesson I learned in tennis years ago.

I started playing tennis when our children were young. I liked the exercise, and it met my need to do something that would bring immediate results from my efforts. I'd practice hitting serves with a bucket of balls. At the beginning of the practice session, maybe only five out of ten serves were good. After an hour, maybe eight out of ten were good. In that season of my life, that measurable progress gave me a sense of accomplishment I couldn't find in the endless tasks of changing diapers, wiping peanut butter off countertops, and sorting laundry.

So I practiced tennis when I could and took lessons from a tough coach who noticed the minute I started getting sloppy or gave in to fatigue.

"Carol!" she'd yell across the tennis court. "Stay focused. Back to basics!"

I always knew what she meant. Fatigue—that horrible I'm-at-my-limit feeling—was causing me to forget what I knew to be important: eye on the ball; body in position; hit the ball in the middle of the racquet; follow through. Good tennis players remember the basics, regardless of feelings. And holding on is what leads to results—positive improvement.

The same is true in parenting.

We know most of the basics. In fact, we're able to remember or discern what's important . . . when it comes to someone else's children. But when it comes to parenting our own children, our feelings often get in the way of doing the right thing. It's those "heart attacks" that so often conflict with head knowledge.

We know that our goal is to raise children with strong character who are capable of coping and making good choices. We know that loving and letting go is the way to reach that goal and meet our children's needs for healthy independence. We know we have to teach them to be responsible for their lives and allow them to face the consequences of their choices and actions. But sometimes our fatigue or our desire to protect or our desire for a short-term, feel-good quick fix is greater than our determination to let them learn the long-term lesson. We don't want to wait around while they struggle to discover the lesson—while the nine-month-old cries himself to sleep; while the preschooler learns to stand up for herself when someone takes her toys; while the sixth grader learns to go to a teacher for help.

Sometimes we don't have the patience to listen or put a foot down, like when I gave my whining kids the package of cookies from the shelf in the grocery store. Sometimes our desire to be kind and tender wins out.

I'm reminded of the interview I had with a psychologist and recognized parenting expert who is also a mother. She knew all the answers. From cleaning their plates to carrying out the garbage, she knew how to make children accept their responsibilities. She made it all sound so simple.

Finally, feeling like a complete failure as a mother, I put down my pencil and asked, "Does all this really work for you at home with your own children?"

"Of course not," she smiled. "When they are your own kids, all too often your mother heart takes over for your head knowledge. But you usually know when that's happening, so you stop and remind yourself to go back to what you know."

Back to basics.

FOR REFLECTION

1. Letting go is a key concept in coping with life's everyday challenges. Other than in your parenting, where have you had to choose to let go of something? How can you compare this example to the process of letting go of your children?

2. "We let go because we love our children." What does this mean to you?

3. What are some of the consequences of overprotecting your children?

4. "We let go for our own good." What does this mean to you?

5. Can you think of a recent example in your parenting when you settled for a quick-fix solution rather than a long-term one? How would the situation have been different if you had been thinking of long-term goals?

PONDERPOINT

INDEPENDENCE DAY

On my first day in the first grade, I panicked and cried and raced back to the car where my mother was, ran top speed. . . .

"Mama! Take me home!"

I thought she would be so happy to see me and to discover my undiminished need of her presence, her love and her protection. I sat smiling in the front seat and heard the car's ignition even before she turned the key. She never turned the key.

Only now do I understand her own tears as she took my hand and walked me back into the school again.

"Mama, do you hate me?"

"No! Not at all. I love you — "

What she was saying was, "Go away from me — in order to be."

So here I am, all done with first grade and writing books like any independent adult, and it is done. My mother sorrowed in the separation, but I am, by miracle, her joy and her accomplishment. Both. It is an astonishing act of love.

WALTER WANGERIN JR., *MEASURING THE DAYS*[10]

3

Control and Surrender

> Hold all loosely, so it does not hurt
> when God pries your fingers away.
>
> CORRIE TEN BOOM

HELPLESS SURRENDER

Sunday morning, March 22, 1981. It is a day indelibly marked in my memory. We thought nine-year-old Derek had been coming down with the flu the night before, because he kept throwing up. He spent a restless night on a puffy comforter on the floor by our bed, the privileged spot reserved for sick children in our family. He was in and out of the bathroom all night long, and by dawn, he looked frighteningly pale and dehydrated. He kept whimpering for something to drink, but even sucking an ice cube triggered his retching again.

I hated to bother the doctor on a Sunday morning, but obviously this child needed something to stop his throwing up. When I reached our pediatrician, he asked a few seemingly routine questions and told me to meet him at his office in half an hour. "And," he instructed, "bring along a urine sample." No problem. Derek was going to the bathroom often.

Lynn and the two girls went off to Sunday school, and I told them we'd be home before they got back.

When we got to the doctor's office, I helped Derek out of the car. He seemed so weak and suddenly thinner. The doctor met us at the door, put us in an examining room, and took the urine specimen down the hall to a lab. I heard the clinking of instruments and then his approaching footsteps, which echoed eerily in the empty office. He joined us and looked down at Derek, who was crumpled in a heap on the examining table.

"We have diabetes here," he announced quietly. "You need to get him to the hospital immediately. I'll call ahead so they will be ready to start an IV to stabilize him." His next words were muffled by the first numbing waves of shock sweeping over me, momentarily protecting me from the pain of comprehending.

Diabetes. As the word swirled through my head, visions of frail sickly victims flashed across my mind. Lynn's cousin, who was in his twenties, had recently died of the disease. The word had nothing to do with Derek, a normally athletic, energetic, healthy child.

Within minutes we were on our way out of the doctor's office. I had come in thinking Derek had the flu, expecting to get some medicine and some advice. Instead we were rushing to the hospital with something incurable and potentially life threatening. For the first time, I couldn't get a prescription for my child; there was no cure.

Eventually I reached Lynn by phone, and he joined me at the hospital. The next several hours were a blur, but slowly the impact of the diagnosis sank in as the doctor and nurses answered our questions and explained what diabetes would mean in Derek's life.

For some reason Derek's pancreas no longer produced sufficient insulin to meet his body's needs. He would have to take insulin injections every day to survive. He would also have to follow a strict diet and carefully balance his food intake with regular exercise. We would have to monitor his control with daily blood tests and learn to detect and deal with the inevitable and frightening insulin reactions. In spite of these precautions, Derek still faced the threat of complications such as blindness, kidney failure, or heart problems. The information seemed overwhelming.

Our little boy lay quietly on the bed as the doctor spoke. Although the IV solution was slowly giving him strength, he didn't yet comprehend the meaning of all this. Maybe, just for now, we could protect him from the painful realization that diabetes might rob him of his carefree childhood and endanger his future.

Later that night, Lynn and I sat holding hands beside Derek's hospital bed. It had been an emotionally exhausting day, and we ached as we looked at our sleeping child anchored to his bed by the tubes running into his body. He looked so young and helpless.

We felt helpless too, aware for the first time of our inability to control Derek's future.

"Let's pray," Lynn said, so we knelt by that hospital bed, and quietly we prayed, surrendering our child to the Lord. As well as I can remember, this was our prayer:

> Lord, we've always had trouble believing that you love our children more than we do and that you will take care of them. We know we've tried to control their lives. But Lord, for the first time, we face a problem with no human solution. We can't cure it or change it. So we come to you in humble dependence and place this child in your hands tonight. We know you have a plan for his life. Please take care of him and help us to accept that plan with trust and loving support. Amen.

That night, we surrendered out of our helplessness, but in the days, months, and years since, we've experienced how God provides what we need in the wake of that kind of surrender. He's given us the peace and strength to face the subsequent challenges of letting go, as we vowed to encourage Derek to lead a normal life in spite of his disease—to jet off to another state with his jump-rope demonstration team a few weeks later; to run a six-mile race two months later; eventually to play high school sports and go off to college in another state.

"God isn't completely free to work in a child's life until we let go of that child and leave him or her entirely in God's hands," writes author Margie Lewis.[1]

INTENTIONAL SURRENDER

That night in the hospital was certainly a turning point in Derek's life. It was also a turning point in the life of this mother who likes to be in control. From that moment forward, I had a choice: hold this child tightly and protectively, or more loosely, with faith and trust that God would provide. It's a choice I had to make. Every day. Choice by choice. One way would stifle his growth and paralyze him with dependence; the other would allow him to grow and go. The right choice depends upon a daily attitude of surrender, and, I keep learning, that same choice applies to everything in life that I treasure.

Think of it this way. We all have treasures. Things that are valuable to us. Our children are the treasures of our hearts. We love them with a powerful love that words fail to describe. Consider what we do with our most valuable treasures. The more we value something, the more we worry about that something might happen to it, and the tighter we wrap our fingers around it. That's why we put our jewelry in safe-deposit boxes and install alarm systems in our homes and cars. We want to protect our valuable treasures.

Because we value our children more than jewels or cars, we're even more tempted to wrap our fingers around them tightly. We want to protect them and to protect ourselves from the fear of losing them. We choose to relax our fingers and surrender our children to God, but living out that choice requires faith and trust in God—that he is in control and will do what he promises. Surrendering is an attitude of the heart before it is an action of the hand. Surrendering involves recognizing that we don't own our children.

In our heads, we know that to be true, and yet from the moment a child is born, we develop a subtle attitude of ownership. We choose the child's name carefully, consulting all those little books that give the meanings of names, and we pick one that fits our dream for our child. The child gets our last name, which makes him or her part of our family. We bask in the compliments that "he's got your eyes" or "she has your smile."

> *Surrendering is an attitude of the heart before it is an action of the hand.*

We are totally responsible for our newborns, and they are totally dependent upon us for everything. We dress them in the clothes we want them to wear. We give them what we want them to eat. We talk about "*my* child this . . ." and "*my* child that . . ." When the children's choir sings at church, we proudly point to the third one over from the left on the second row. "That's *my* child!" we tell the person sitting next to us. No wonder the word *my* takes on a deeper meaning.

And yet, as Christian parents we must again and again—daily, even hourly—remember that our children are God's, not ours. In mothering, as in all areas of life, we are stewards of God's gifts. This means that:

- All that we have is entrusted to us from God.
- God gives us the privilege and responsibility of caring for all that is entrusted to us, our talents, time, money, homes—and, yes, our children.
- God asks us to hold that which is entrusted to us loosely, being willing to surrender our children to him with gratitude

for his goodness and with faith in his good purposes. Surrender is first and foremost a heart attitude.

In her book *Mother Dance,* Dr. Harriet Lerner notes the negative overtones of the word *surrender,* acknowledging that it is ultimately a necessary and positive—though painful—action. "Surrender has connotations of giving up, failing, rather than of giving ourselves over to forces or events larger than we are."[2]

A STORY OF SURRENDER IN GRATITUDE

In 1 Samuel 1–2, a mother named Hannah illustrates this attitude of surrender from the moment her child was conceived. Hannah was barren, a painful stigma for a Hebrew wife. In her anguish and with great faith, she prayed that God would give her a son. Her prayer included a promise: if God gifted her with a son, she would relinquish the boy to God's service all the days of his life. In time God answered her prayer, and Hannah had a son she named Samuel, meaning "heard of God," because God answered her prayer.

For a few short years Hannah devoted herself to the physical love and care of her precious baby, nurturing and then weaning him. (The word *nurture* comes from nursing, which illustrates an important point here that we must nurture before we can wean; we must love before we let go.) Because of her care in the critical early years of Samuel's character development, this mother's indelible imprint remained in him, and he began to make a difference for the Lord, even as a child.

After the boy was weaned, probably about age three, she took him, as she had promised, to the temple to live in the service of the Lord with Eli the priest.

As she left him Hannah prayed a prayer of praise and gratitude that amazes me. Surely her heart was broken, knowing she might not see this child again for a year. (She was not simply sending a child to half-day kindergarten.) He was her heart's treasure. What a sacrifice! Yet in her gratitude for the gift given her by God, she could say, "My heart rejoices in the LORD; in the LORD my horn [strength] is lifted high" (1 Sam. 2:1).

Of course, this physical relinquishment of a child is nearly impossible to imagine. (Then again, there were days when I would have gladly gone to the church and given my three-year-old to the pastor!) But the underlying con-cept is clear: we live out the recognition that our children are not our own but are lives entrusted to us from God, lives we must hold lightly, lives we relinquish to him, at least in our hearts.

> *Our children are not our own but are lives entrusted to us from God, lives we relinquish to him.*

Surely Hannah didn't feel she'd given this child all she could. She didn't feel she was done with mothering, and yet she trusted God to be there for her son, to finish the process. Gien Karssen, author of *Her Name Is Woman*, a book of sketches of biblical women, notes that Hannah's dedication was "radical in nature" because "she had to offer Samuel to God daily, trusting Him to protect Samuel's faith in the midst of the corruption" in the temple.[3] Don't we all face similar challenges as we imprint our love and values into our children's hearts when they are young and then offer them to God, trusting him to protect them in the midst of corruption in the world?

There's a bit more to Hannah's story.

Each year his mother made him a little robe and took it to him when she went up with her husband to offer the annual sacrifice. Eli [the priest] would bless Elkanah and his wife [Hannah], saying, "May the LORD give you children by this woman to take the place of the one she prayed for and gave to the LORD." Then they would go home. And the LORD was gracious to Hannah; she conceived and gave

birth to three sons and two daughters. Meanwhile, the boy
Samuel grew up in the presence of the LORD.

1 Samuel 2:19–21

This touching detail, making him a coat each year, is a
reminder of one of the basic guidelines of letting go from chapter 1. As Hannah released her child, after weaning him and placing him in Eli's care, she began to change the way she expressed
her love for him. Yet her feelings remained steady and strong.

Also, lovingly yet painfully relinquishing her child to God with
gratitude, Hannah discovered that one can never outgive God.
She was blessed with five more children, and she had the joy of
seeing Samuel grow up to be a godly man who listened and
responded to God.

A STORY OF SURRENDER IN FAITH

In the Bible there's another story of a parent that is particularly powerful to me. This parent's journey to surrender has
become the model for so many of my struggles with loving and
letting go, especially of my children. I followed in this parent's
footprints as I learned to deal with Derek's diabetes and his
unknown future. I've followed in them again and again in learning to let go. The parent's name is Abraham.

PARENTS' TREASURE

Abraham was one hundred years old and his wife Sarah was
ninety when God promised them a son.

"Laughable," Sarah said, in effect, when she heard the news.
"Surely not possible. I don't see how."

"Is anything too hard for the LORD?" God's messenger asked,
a rhetorical question that still echoes through the centuries to any
of us who question whether God will do as he promises. Of
course nothing is too hard for the Lord, and he has a plan for
each of our children, as surely as he has a plan for us: to give us

a future and a hope (Jer. 29:11). All God asks in return is that we trust him and hold our treasures loosely, not tightly, surrendering them to him. Our trust in him must be greater than our fears for our children. God must remain first in our hearts.

Abraham demonstrated that faith, first in believing God's promise that he would be a parent.

> Without weakening in his faith, he faced the fact that his body was as good as dead—since he was about a hundred years old—and that Sarah's womb was also dead. Yet he did not waver through unbelief regarding the promise of God, but was strengthened in his faith and gave glory to God, being fully persuaded that God had power to do what he had promised.
>
> *Romans 4:19–21*

Abraham was rewarded for his faith with a son, Isaac, by his wife Sarah.

We can only imagine how Abraham loved this son he had waited so long to have. From the moment Abraham held Isaac, the baby became the idol of his heart. As the child grew, so did Abraham's love. They bonded closer and closer as Abraham cared for his child. Did his love for his son grow stronger than his trust in God? Did Abraham get his priorities mixed up? Did he unwittingly put Isaac first in his heart?

A FATHER'S TEST

Is that why God commanded Abraham to take his son Isaac to Mount Moriah and sacrifice him there? We know that God never intended Abraham to sacrifice his son, for God does not approve of child sacrifices. And surely this was not a test to prove something to God, for God knows everything. But maybe this was a test to reveal something to Abraham about himself and the priorities of his heart.

In spite of his feelings, Abraham could not argue with the Lord's command. He knew this son was a gift from God and not his possession. Because of his faith, Abraham obeyed. He saddled his donkey, took his son, a knife, and the wood to start the fire, and traveled three days to Mount Moriah. In spite of the painful conflict between what he knew in his head and what he felt in his heart, Abraham kept trudging up the mountain. How he must have agonized over his fears about his son's unknown future, but he trusted that God was sufficient and would provide, even if Abraham's worst fears were realized.

When he and Isaac got to the top of Mount Moriah, Abraham built an altar, arranged the wood, bound the boy, and laid him on the altar. Just as Abraham was ready to plunge the knife into his son, the Lord stopped him and said, "Because you have done this, and have not withheld your son, your only son, I will indeed bless you" (Gen. 22:16–17 RSV).

The test was complete. Abraham's trust had been revealed. As A. W. Tozer writes:

> God let the suffering old man go through with it up to the point where he knew there would be no retreat and then forbade him to lay a hand upon the boy. To the wondering patriarch he now says in effect, "It's all right, Abraham. I never intended you should actually slay the lad. I only wanted to remove him from the temple of your heart that I might reign unchallenged there. I wanted to correct the perversion that existed in your love. Now you may have the boy, sound and well."[4]

GOD'S PROMISE

The Bible tells us that when Abraham stopped, his knife in his hand, he looked over and saw a ram in a thicket, caught by its horns. Realizing that God had provided a substitute sacrifice that day, Abraham offered the ram instead of his son. Then Abraham called that place Jehovah Jireh, which means "the Lord will provide."

That promise is ours forever and means that when we trudge up Mount Moriah in our own lives and reach that place of surrender with our treasures, we will experience the same blessing. We will discover that God provides what we need when we surrender to him whatever we hold tightly in our hands.

This promise has been foundational to my faith. I've learned its application through my mothering, but I've also had to apply it to all of my life. Whenever I hold on to something too tightly—my desire for success or affirmation or recognition or my fears about my child's future—God calls me back up Mount Moriah. "Come. Bring me what you are holding so tightly in your hand. Loosen your grip on your way up. Bring it as your offering. Surrender it to me. Trust me." And back I go, trudging up that familiar mountain again, following in Abraham's footprints to that place of surrender with my offering in my clenched hand.

> *God provides what we need when we surrender to him whatever we hold tightly in our hands.*

Sometimes I turn around before I get there.

"No, Lord, I know best what this child needs—and these are the wrong circumstances."

Or, "I don't believe you can possibly love this child more than I do."

Or, "My way is not your way, Lord. And I want my way. I want to be in control."

Or, "No, this child—this treasure—is *mine*, Lord."

But even if I take a detour, I eventually find myself back on that mountain path of surrender, the offering still in my hand with a slightly loosened grip. All the way up the mountain, I keep prying my fingers looser and looser until I reach the very top with an open hand. There I surrender my offering to God in trust and receive his provision of peace and comfort. Always.

Jehovah Jireh: God will provide . . . when we surrender our treasures to him. That's his promise. And he will meet our needs. Even if we have to face our greatest fears.

A Birthday Present

For my fiftieth birthday recently, my husband, Lynn, surprised me with the most meaningful birthday gift I've ever received. He gathered the family and planned a party at a restaurant in a nearby little town known for its art galleries. In fact we have friends who own a gallery there. After having lunch and wandering around the town a bit, we ended up in our friends' gallery.

Though we like art, we are not owners of any great art. Instead many spots of honor on our shelves at home still have lumps of clay fashioned into treasures by chubby little hands many years ago.

We walked around the gallery that day and oohed and ahhed over many of the pieces. Then as I turned a corner, I spotted a mound of something covered by a cloth and a big bow with a huge card that said, "Happy Birthday, Carol." I stopped short, suddenly knowing exactly what was under that cloth. Years earlier I had seen a bronze sculpture of Abraham holding up Isaac, the treasure of his heart, with an adoring look on his face. I told Lynn then that of all the pieces of art in the whole wide world, this would be the one I'd love to own.

Lynn lifted off the cloth and there was the sculpture I had longed for.

Many tears later, I helped pack that precious fifty-pound sculpture in our car. And it now holds a central place of honor in our home. It's on a table where I can see it from my kitchen stool early in the morning. I sip my coffee and talk to God while the sun comes up, and when the sunlight catches the amazing details of the sculpture, I'm always reminded to surrender the treasures of my heart to God as the first order of the day.

Because I am not in control.

He is.

Because my children are not mine but are entrusted to my care, for a season.

And so I pray:

Help me, God, to know how to appreciate them, relinquish them, and love them in a way that honors you, who promises a future and a hope.

FOR REFLECTION

1. We are called both to love and to let go of our children. What is the difference between loving and letting go in this sense, and what are some examples of each in your parenting?

2. What would a prayer of gratitude for your child say? Try to write such a prayer (or discuss the prayer's content, if you are with a group). Could you write such a prayer even if you were at a painful point in your letting-go journey?

3. "God isn't completely free to work in a child's life until we let go of that child and leave him or her entirely in God's hands," writes author Margie Lewis. What does this mean for you at this particular stage of your child's life?

4. What treasure have you surrendered recently? What are you being nudged to surrender now? How will you do this?

5. If you were to identify a piece of sculpture or a painting that represents some aspect of your parental joy or pain, what would the image be?

PONDERPOINT

LET GO AND LET GOD

As children bring their broken toys
with tears for us to mend,
I brought my broken dreams to God
because he is my friend.
But then instead of leaving him
in peace to work alone,
I hung around and tried to help
with ways that were my own.
At last I snatched them back and cried,
"How can you be so slow?"
"My child," he said, "what could I do?
You never did let go."

ANONYMOUS

4

Overcoming Mommy Fears

> I pray as if it depended upon God,
> but I act as if it depended upon me.
>
> MOTHER TERESA

When it comes to my children, I like to be in control of their lives. I like to be the Fixer of Their Problems, Maker of Dreams Come True, and Creator of Happily Ever Afters. I like to think that I can keep them safe and happy. Always. That's why I can relate to this honest admission by Judith Viorst, mother of three sons:

> I once was positive that as long as I was right there, my sons couldn't choke to death on a piece of meat. Why? Because I knew that I would keep nagging them to take smaller bites and chew carefully. And I also knew that if worse really came to worst, I would seize a knife and perform a tracheotomy. Like many mothers, I saw myself—and in some ways still see myself—as their guardian angel.[1]

Of course, we can't always control their lives or fix their problems, which causes us to face one of the greatest barriers to letting go: our Mommy Fears. Mommy Fears are those mostly irrational but real worries about all the worst-case possibilities that might happen to our children. Mommy Fears grow bigger in our heads the more we think about them and cause us to do things we shouldn't. Like overreact. Or hold on when we should let go. They give us "yikes attacks."

Those fears can also affect the choices we make for our children. Here's one woman's analysis of her parents' response to her request to take trumpet lessons in elementary school:

> If you take trumpet lessons, you'll want to play in the high school band. And if you play in the high school band, you'll have to travel to games. And if you travel to games, you'll want to ride in the school bus with all your friends, and we don't know anything at all about the bus driver. So, no, you can't take trumpet lessons.[2]

Mommy Fears often start the minute we know we're pregnant. I recently heard the term "womb doom" and instantly understood the meaning. I used to worry that something I did or didn't do while my children were in the womb might have doomed them before they were born. Did I eat the right foods, listen to the right music, stay stress free and in the right state of mind?

After they're born we start worrying about whether they're getting enough to eat (counting the number of wet diapers), breathing through the night (getting up to check when they are too quiet), progressing developmentally as they should (noting whether they turn over as quickly as my friend's baby does). Later we worry whether they will be potty trained in time to start preschool, will look both ways before crossing, will make good choices, and will always remember what we've told them to do when we're not around to remind them . . . to buckle up, wear a bike helmet, and just say no.

Our fears often become obstacles to letting go. They control our responses, and therefore our children's choices, just as in the example about taking trumpet lessons. A nine-year-old wants to sleep over at her friend's house. We know the parents, but we still worry. Do we let her go? A son wants to play football, but we fear possible injury. Do we let him play? A teenager dreams of becoming a pilot ... or missionary ... or forest-fire fighter, but we fear the sacrifices those dreams demand. A high school junior wants to go off to college in another state, but we fear that might mean meeting and marrying someone from far away and never coming home again. Does our desire to protect them (and indirectly ourselves) interfere with our willingness to encourage rather than discourage our children?

When do we hold on, and when do we let go? When do we say yes, and when do we say no? Where is that fine line between being wisely protective and being overprotective? To sort through these mind-boggling questions, I use a process I call the Mommy Fears Formula.

I learned this simple process one summer when I faced a bunch of Mommy Fears every Saturday morning. Lindsay was ten years old and into horses, big time. Because we lived in the country and because I grew up around horses and because we thought horses and 4-H were healthy outlets for children, Lindsay had a horse. Only one problem. In spite of my experience, horses scare me. They weigh about twelve hundred pounds, wear sharp steel shoes on all four feet, and when something spooks them, they can rear up and flail the air with their hooves.

Every Saturday morning, Lindsay and I would hitch our horse trailer up to the car, load her horse, bolt the trailer doors, and drive about twenty miles to the county fairgrounds for 4-H horse shows. This meant driving the horse and trailer through busy intersections, over bumpy railroad tracks, and down highways where you're supposed to go real fast, at least forty miles an hour, or drivers behind you get mad. Every Saturday, I woke up filled with Mommy Fears. What if we don't hook up the trailer just right and it becomes unhitched when we're zooming down the highway? What if the horse tips over inside the trailer when we go around a corner? What if the back door on the trailer flies open when we go across the railroad tracks, and the horse falls out? My what-if fears grew bigger and bigger, and I questioned why in tarnation I ever got myself into this spot. And then I remembered. It's because Lindsay loves horses, and I should not let my Mommy Fears get in the way of allowing her to grow into the person God created her to be. Still, I dreaded our drives to the fairgrounds.

"Mom, you worry too much," Lindsay told me one Saturday as I sat with my white-knuckled hands clenching the steering wheel. Of course she was right, and I knew I had to unclench my hand and give my Mommy Fears to God.

PRAYERFUL PROCESS

That day, as Lindsay rode her horse around the fairgrounds, I thought about other mothers and how they deal with their Mommy Fears. I remembered Jochebed in the Bible, the mother of baby Moses, who was born during a dark time in Israel's history when the Pharoah ordered the drowning of all male Jewish babies. In an attempt to spare her son's life, Jochebed carefully made a waterproof basket, gently laid her son in it, and let him go, floating down the Nile River into an unknown future. Surely she was filled with Mommy Fears about his safety and his destination, but she did all she could to protect her child, and then she had to let him go, trusting that God would provide. As the story goes, God did provide. Pharaoh's daughter found baby Moses, took him home, and brought him up, even allowing Jochebed to nurse him until he was weaned.

I decided that, like Jochebed, I needed to look my fear right square in the face and deal with it. I needed to place it in my hand and consider all the parts of that fear. I needed to sort out the ones I could do something about from the ones I couldn't control. Jochebed built the safest, best basket possible. That was her human contribution. When it came to driving the horse trailer, I could make sure the car and trailer were in good repair, with decent tires, brakes, and a strong hitch. I could go through the hitch-up process carefully, making sure we got it right. I could double-check the latch on the back door.

I do what I can do. Now what's left of this fear are the parts I can't control. The what ifs of accidents or circumstances are out of my control, and I lift those to God in a prayer.

I do the possible and leave the impossible to God

Over the years, this prayerful process—my Mommy Fears Formula—has helped me face and sort through my Mommy Fears. Concerning fears about accidents and my children's safety, I can purchase the best car seat available and be sure they're buckled up. I can purchase safety gates and outlet plugs and special latches for all the cabinets. I can make sure they wear bike helmets. Those are the possible parts. Then I turn the impossibles into a prayer.

> *I do the possible and leave the impossible to God.*

This process turns on one central understanding: there are things in my life I cannot control. The world around us tells us that we can and should take control of our lives; that knowledge is power and we can do anything we want to do and be anything we want to be, if we just work hard enough or try hard enough. The world tells us that if we are bold enough or determined enough, life is risk free. As one commentator laments, "The idea that our individual lives and the nation's life can and should be risk free has grown to be an obsession, driven far and deep into American attitudes."[3]

Talking specifically in terms of parenting, Dr. Harriet Lerner, author of *Mother Dance*, writes,

It's the American way to believe that every problem has a solution and every obstacle can be overcome. . . . When things get rough, we can try harder, make a new plan, think positively, and bootstrap our way to success. . . . Much of the pain and grief that mothers feel stems from the belief that we should have control over our children, when it is hard enough to have control over ourselves.[4]

Yet no matter how hard we try or how long we work at this control issue, life eventually hands us or our children a circumstance we can't control, and we dramatically learn another of God's foundational truths.

Ultimately there are things in our children's lives we can't control either.

I learned this with Derek's diabetes, a life-threatening disease that has at times threatened to steal my peace of mind and overwhelm me with fear. To get a handle on my fears about his future, I used the Mommy Fears Formula. I could make sure he had the supplies he needed: insulin and snacks and juice and blood tester. As long as I was in charge, I could make sure he ate the right foods. I could take him to the doctor for regular checkups and encourage him through hard times. But the long-range complications and accidents, such as getting separated from a source of insulin and sugar? I knew I couldn't always control those circumstances, and I had to turn them into a prayer to God, knowing that even if I faced my worst fear, God would provide. He promises that his Word is a lamp to our feet. When we stand on his promises, he holds up just enough light for us to take the next step. And then the next step. One step at a time.

> *"God, grant me the serenity to accept the things I cannot change, the courage to change the things I can, and the wisdom to know the difference."*
> *Reinhold Niebuhr*

Over and over again, this prayerful Mommy Fears Formula shows me a way out of the Mommy Fears that threaten to control me—and my children.

ONE MOTHER'S STORY

My worst fear is that I might lose a child. I'm not alone. A friend told me she could not truly let go of her children until she reached a maturity of faith that enabled her to claim the promise of Romans 8:28: "in all things God works for the good of those who love him, who have been called according to his purpose."

She finally translated that verse to mean that even if her son were struck by lightning on his way to school or even if her daughter had a terminal disease, she would be able to survive the horrible circumstances because God would give her what she needed to get through it. That would be the "good" in the promise that God would work for good.

If something happened to one of our children, could I pick up the pieces and go on? In faith, could I claim God's promise in Romans 8:28?

One of the ways I find an answer to those questions is to turn to parents who have lived through the nightmare of losing a child. I look at them, knowing their experience could be my experience, and in their responses, I search for the assurance that I, too, could cope with my worst fear.

A friend faced this horror. She says her daily challenge now is to make sense out of life without her only son, who was killed on a clear cold December afternoon. She had casually said goodbye that afternoon to seventeen-year-old Kurt as he and a friend went goose hunting. She reminded him to be home before dark. Her husband was out of town and her daughter away at college, so she and Kurt, just the two of them, were going to a favorite restaurant for dinner. A special treat together.

The time passed quickly that afternoon, but she remembers looking at the clock close to five and feeling that familiar twinge of fear she'd had since her children were toddlers. At dark she always wanted her family to gather into the safety of home.

And then the phone rang. It was the call she'd dreaded all her life. "There has been an accident," the voice said. Her son . . . hit by a car . . . confusion of details. . . . Finally, the instructions: "Come to the hospital immediately."

She got there quickly, but it was too late. Kurt was dead, and she walked into a nightmare, trying to pick up the pieces. In the next days and weeks, she set aside time to journal her journey through despair, writing down her feelings, memories, and prayers, an open-hearted, broken-hearted conversation with a loving God. She wrote about the pain.

> I feel I have a lifetime of love left for him and I don't know what to do with it. My heart is truly broken. I feel like I'm in a great ocean and you, God, are holding my head above the water, and my friends have ahold of my hands, but I'm not able to come up because of the rock of sorrow that's tied to my ankles. The loss is so deep, there is no bottom.

She described her connected losses: because Kurt had been the only child at home, she suddenly lost her role as a mother.

> You plan to separate from your children as they build their own lives and families, but the finality of death before you're ready is so hard to take.

> My whole life for the last twenty years has been at home, trying to teach my children right from wrong and what is pleasing in God's eyes, and in mine too. I feel a great need to focus my life in some new direction. My family really needs very little of me anymore.

She wrote about regrets, feeling she had worried too much and missed some of the joy of living with Kurt.

A mother's sense of responsibility is to guide, discipline, and shape, so she sometimes lacks the freedom to enjoy the child's exuberant gifts. Kurt's gifts were so apparent to others who approached him positively. Because of my anxiety, maybe I missed some of the joy of knowing him. I've always been an anxious mother, and it's a hard habit to break. Feelings can be so powerful. It was hard releasing him to grow up, to let God take some of the care.

She was surprised that she wasn't freed from that worry even after Kurt's death. Yet she sensed God leading her somewhere through the shadows of fear and doubt.

I don't know why. Nothing in this life can hurt him anymore. [God,] help my heart to believe and know that he is okay, that he is resting in your love. I know you are teaching me to trust. I feel like I trusted you completely with my life, but now I know it wasn't an absolute trust. Help me to trust completely and learn your will for my life.

She could see she hadn't truly released Kurt to the Lord's loving protection even after death. A few weeks after the accident, a thoughtful friend brought her a rose. A simple gesture, it took on deep significance because Kurt had sometimes given her roses: one for her birthday and two on his last Valentine's Day. He'd try to surprise her, and she'd always been deeply touched.

She sensed that this rose, delivered by her friend, was sent by Kurt and God for a purpose. And with fresh courage, she made her first trip back to the cemetery—to place the rose on Kurt's grave. Before she went, she wrote a line to Kurt: "It will symbolize God's great gift of you and my release of you into his care."

It was New Year's Day. She drove to the cemetery alone and sat on the fresh grave. She thought, prayed, and finally wrote,

Our children never really belong to us. They are God's from the beginning and only loaned to us for whatever length of time and whatever eternal purpose God has in mind. And yet, they are truly a part of our very life and being. Losing one is worse than losing an arm or leg. Only trusting that God is their true source and true ending can bring any peace of mind. Trust and faith are tested to the utmost. May my faith and trust be strengthened.

I return what was never really mine but still a part of me—a very part of my body after conception. After birth all we ever really have are images and memories from moment to moment when loved ones are out of sight. It's funny that the moment and memories never seem so important until you know the time to build any more has passed. Let me see the importance of each moment, cherish each special time.

I miss him terribly and know there will always be a part of me missing, but I know you have something more planned for my life. I thank you for using Kurt's life and death for good. Please use mine to your glory; let me serve you in whatever way, grand or small.

That day, she released her son to the Lord. She still has a broken heart. She still knows she will never be the same person she was before she received that phone call. But in her journey through despair, she sees familiar Scripture passages in a new light.

"In all things God works for the good." *Maybe the good won't be tomorrow or even next year. Maybe the good will be in eternity, she thinks.*

"Weeping may tarry for the night, but joy comes with the morning" (Ps. 30:5 RSV). Maybe the joy won't be the kind she's known before. Maybe it will be something new, different. In her diary, she concludes,

Love costs, but it's worth the price. Having Kurt in my life for seventeen years is worth every minute of the pain I feel now. His life was a precious gift; his presence an irreplaceable treasure. He is safely home, and God will help me complete my journey here.

Kurt's mother is on a journey of growth. Having faced her worst fear, she in faith believed that God had remained faithful through her loss. Like Job in the Old Testament, who had lost his children and his wealth, she could say, "The LORD gave and the LORD has taken away; may the name of the LORD be praised" (Job 1:21).

LET THEM GO AND GROW WITH CONFIDENCE

At one time or another, we all struggle with Mommy Fears. Some are huge, like the fear of losing a child to death. Others are part of the daily routine. Are we making the right choices for our children? Should we allow them to go to the amusement park with another family, take the bus to town, go to a movie with friends, go skiing with the neighbors? We feel anxious as we watch them jump off the high-diving board, drive off in a friend's car, or pack up for the Boy Scout camping trip. All of these activities involve some risk. Each one brings to mind some story about a terrible accident, and we find ourselves faced again with fears. These fears tempt us to try to control their environment or limit their experiences and therefore their growth.

Parenting is risky. We have to accept the results of the decisions we make or the actions we take or don't take with our children. For weeks Kurt's mother agonized over her decision to let him go hunting that afternoon. What if she had said no? What if she had told him to be home earlier? Yet she began to see the futility of reliving the event, and she knew she hadn't caused the accident to happen. Prayerfully she had to let go of that guilt.

I know one mother who sends her children out the door, mentally dressing them in the whole armor of God as described vividly in Ephesians 6:10–20. She claims the promise of protection by giving each child the belt of truth, the breastplate of righteousness, shoes of readiness, the shield of faith, the helmet of salvation, and the sword of the Spirit. Still another mother prays for angels to surround her children.

"Every time I send my daughter out the door for the ski team racing practice, my heart is in my throat," a friend told me. "But I just have to remember: There is something I can do. I can always pray."

> *Worrying is taking on a responsibility that belongs to God.*

In *Letters and Papers from Prison,* Dietrich Bonhoeffer writes, "From the moment we wake until we fall asleep we must commend other people wholly and unreservedly to God and leave them in his hands, and transform our anxiety for them into prayers on their behalf."[5]

Our Mommy Fears are real, but when we get tangled up in them, we're showing a lack of trust. We're choosing fear over faith. Worrying is taking on a responsibility that belongs to God. Anxiety is the opposite of faith. When I start wallowing in my worries, I think back to what God has shown me in the midst of my greatest Mommy Fears. The first afternoon nine-year-old Derek was in the hospital with diabetes, a friend called. "I know this may sound funny," she said, "but I almost envy you the journey you're about to embark on with the Lord."

It sounded absolutely absurd at the time, but I now know what she meant. We are most dependent on God in times of crisis. In a journey through despair, we are most aware of our need to trust him, and we're most aware of his comforting presence.

I am not thankful Derek has diabetes, but I am thankful the Lord has given him the courage to accept it, the strength to deal with the added responsibilities, and the maturing faith not to fear the future. Today I am also thankful that God is using these circumstances to shape this child into a young man with deep compassion and a desire to help other people.

I have to remember this when the Mommy Fears threaten to become a stumbling block to letting my children grow and go with confidence.

In writing about preparing for parental release, Miriam Huffman Rockness notes the truths found in Philippians 4:6–7: "Do not be anxious about anything, but in everything, by prayer and petition, with thanksgiving, present your requests to God. And the peace of God, which transcends all understanding, will guard your hearts and your minds in Christ Jesus." She writes,

> Simply stated, *our* work is to release our worries with an act of prayer; *God's* work is to guard our hearts and minds with His peace. . . .
>
> Can we be certain our prayers will guarantee our children's physical safety? Not necessarily. Our confidence comes not from the particular answers to our prayers but from the One to whom we pray. We can be sure, however, that God cares more perfectly than we about our children's welfare. Nothing will touch them that has not first passed through the filter of His love.[6]

FOR REFLECTION

1. List at least five of your Mommy Fears.

2. Pick out your biggest one. Place it in your hand. What are the pieces you can do something about? What are the impossible ones? Write a prayer—talk honestly to God—about the impossible ones.

3. Think of one specific way your child showed you that he or she needs you less now than a year ago. What has been your response?

4. Describe a time when you gave your child a choice, even though you feared the consequence of that choice. Do you feel guilt or regret for having done this? If so, what can you do to "take care of" the guilt or regret? Overall, what did you learn from this experience?

PONDERPOINT

PRAYER FOR A MOTHER

When it comes to raising her children, she's bewildered about balance.

She wants to protect them; she wants to teach them how to walk with confidence, not fear.

She wants to give them more than she was given as a girl; she wants them to know what she learned about having to "make do."

She wants to smooth their rocky road; she wants them to be resilient.

God, your Word says, "If any of you lacks wisdom, he should ask God, who gives generously to all without finding fault" (James 1:5). So on her behalf, I pray: Now and for the next ten (make that thirty) years, your parental guidance is requested. Grant her wisdom. Make the rough places plain.

EVELYN BENCE,
PRAYERS FOR GIRLFRIENDS AND SISTERS AND ME[7]

5

Parental Patterns

Living together as a family is meant as much for the refine-
ment, maturation, development of the parent as for the child.
VALERIE BELL, *GETTING OUT OF YOUR KIDS' FACES AND INTO THEIR HEARTS*

When I became a mother, I suddenly looked at my whole life differently, especially my childhood and my relationship with my own mother. I tried to sort through the good and not-so-good parts, deciding what I would keep and what I would definitely do differently. I vowed to make family loyalty just as important as it had been in my own family, and yet I vowed never to make my children feel they had to fulfill my expectations or validate my goodness, because my parents sometimes made me feel that way. I vowed to let my children go their way, even when that was not my way.

In spite of those idealistic, optimistic vows, I sometimes acted unwittingly like my own mother. It's as if there's an inherited attitude buried deep inside me: when it comes to my children, I have a wonderful plan for their lives.

MY WONDERFUL PLAN

Take, for example, my Halloween conflict with Kendall during her kindergarten year. I don't even like Halloween, so I don't know how I got myself tangled in this trauma, except for my desire to be recognized as a good mom. I always felt like the Worst Mother of the Year during the Halloween parade at school. Some kids wore incredibly creative homemade costumes that transformed them into a deck of cards or a banana or whatever hero was hot at the time. I usually sat with the moms of these creations on the bleachers in the gymnasium while they waved wildly and proclaimed proudly, "That's *mine* . . . the Blinking Flashlight . . . right there! I was up until midnight finishing that costume." I'd smile and murmur compliments and then wave as inconspicuously as possible to my kids, who wore things like paper bags over their heads or a football jersey or a wacky pair of sunglasses. In other words, I didn't do Halloween costumes.

One day in October during Kendall's kindergarten, I drove past a store with a big sign: "Custom-Made Halloween Costumes." There in the window was a perfect little red-and-white Orphan Annie outfit. That was the year Annie was hot, and Kendall loved to pretend to be her and sing, "The sun will come out tomorrow . . ." I suddenly got an idea. Kendall's birthday was a few days before Halloween, so I could surprise her with this outfit, which would be perfect for the Halloween parade. What fun!

Before her birthday, I gathered the rest of the costume: white tights, black patent-leather shoes, and a red curly wig. The wig wasn't exactly right, but it was close enough. So I wrapped them up, and on her birthday, Kendall was pleased. Or so I thought. On Halloween morning, I helped her carefully put the whole outfit in a plastic bag.

"I'll be there for the parade," I said and waved as she went out to the school bus. Did I notice that she dragged her feet a bit?

That afternoon, I showed up at school with great anticipation, camera in hand, and went to Kendall's room, where I found her sitting at her desk with the costume crumpled up on her lap. All the other kids ran around the room, squealing with excitement as they got into their costumes.

"I'm not going to wear it, Mom," Kendall announced.

"Kendall, why?" I asked incredulously.

"Because Shelby said the wig is dumb."

"The wig is not dumb!" I tried to persuade her, controlling my frustration with this Shelby who could make my daughter believe her wig was dumb. "It's perfect!"

"I don't want to be in the parade, Mom. Please don't make me." Tears welled up in Kendall's eyes.

I stood there for a moment, critically aware of the conflict of needs here. A few seconds later, I stuffed her costume into the plastic bag.

"Let's go watch the parade," I said, trying to cover up my irritation.

Later, as we drove home in the car, Kendall asked, "Are you mad, Mom?"

"Not mad; mostly sad because you had such a good costume," I told her.

"But it didn't feel good to *me*," she said. "Besides, I wanted to be a cheerleader like Shelby."

"Will you put the costume on when we get home, so I can at least take a picture?"

She agreed, and to this day I have that picture on a wall above my desk. It reminds me that my children are not entrusted to me just to fulfill my expectations or to make me look good or to become a mini version of me. As I've said before, mothering is not all about me.

WHO AM I?

In this long journey of letting go, we need to ask hard questions about who we are and why we're doing what we're doing. We need to look at our patterns of parenting and assess our strengths and vulnerabilities. We do well, as we face the challenge of loving and letting go, to look at who we are at this

> *The "who am I?" question needs to be reexamined, once we become mothers.*

moment in time, both our good and not-so-good parts, and assess how that might affect our willingness or ability to help our children grow toward healthy independence. What needs of our own are we subtly expecting our children to meet? Are our own backgrounds and needs helpful or harmful to our children's growing up? How are our own strengths and weaknesses affecting our parenting? The "who am I?" question needs to be reexamined.

WHAT DO I BRING FROM MY CHILDHOOD FAMILY?

Regardless of its specific form, your childhood family gives you a context or frame of reference through which you interpret your life experience. It was here that you first learned to perceive, react, communicate, trust, evaluate, and interact with others and where you learned who you were in relationship to the world around you.[1]

Becoming parents, or even considering the option of becoming parents, causes us to think about our own childhood—what we learned there, how we were parented, how we reacted to that parenting.

In his book *Your Family Voyage,* Roger Hillerstrom notes a Scripture passage that can help us sort through the helpful and harmful "treasures" that have collected over the years in the family "attic." Hebrews 12:1–2 says, "Let us also lay aside every encumbrance, and the sin which so easily entangles us, and let us run with endurance the race that is set before us, fixing our eyes on Jesus, the author and perfecter of faith" (NASB). Hillerstrom writes:

Sorting through what you've collected in the attic is only the first step of the journey. At some point you must set aside the parts of the family collection that are causing you harm. It doesn't happen all in one day. Often you are able to take only one small box at a time to the garbage heap— only to find, much to your horror, that you run out to the dump to pick through it again. You ask yourself, *"Can I really live without this family 'treasure'? Wait—it's not a treasure, it's fool's gold. And yes, I can live without it."*[2]

Some of our "original family" issues may have ethnic roots. According to Dr. Harriet Lerner in her book *Mother Dance*, different ethnic groups think differently about launching their children:

In a nutshell: White Protestants of British origin place a high premium on children leaving home at the appropriate age, launched into the world as separate, self-reliant and competent individuals. . . . The separateness and independence of family members is so highly prized . . . that in many upper-class WASP communities in the United States, it may be seen as a mark of dysfunction not to send your child to boarding school at least by age 14.

Italian families, in contrast, place the strongest emphasis on family loyalty and togetherness. One doesn't really think of the individual apart from the family, nor of the nuclear family apart from the extended family.[3]

Identifying your family's ethnic and cultural patterns is just one part of sorting through the qualities and characteristics we want to carry on or modify or leave behind. Sometimes such self-examination requires the help of a trained counselor or pastor.

DO I NEED TO BE IN CONTROL?

Some people have a greater need for control than others. Some type A personalities need to make things happen. Others get a sense of importance from controlling their children. People who like to be in control often enjoy their children's baby stage more than the middle school and high school years. Because babies are utterly dependent, we choose what they wear, when and what they eat, where they go, who they go with, and where they sleep. (Notice I didn't say *if* they sleep!) This can give us a false sense of control that can be hard to relinquish. I have a friend who readily admits, "I liked to dress my daughter in bright, color-coordinated outfits. I liked to fix her hair and tell the stylist how to cut it. I'm having a harder time now that she's in seventh grade and choosing her own clothes and doing stuff to her hair that makes me cringe."

But the question many parents, many *mothers,* must answer is posed by psychotherapist Ruth Caplin: "When does something that was absolutely yours stop being part of you—your responsibility, your glory, your pain, yours to control?"[4]

DO I RESIST CHANGE?

Some people accept change easily, but many resist it. Letting go of our growing children demands a change in the way we express our love. As we constantly evaluate where we are in the process, we give our children more freedom and responsibility. A woman came up to me at a recent seminar I was teaching. "I'm frustrated and need some answers. I get along just fine with my four-year-old, but I simply can't cope with my fourteen-year-old. What's the difference? I'm the same mom."

This may be the problem. We can't be the same mom to a fourteen-year-old that we are to a four-year-old. We can't show our love to both children in the same way. We don't have the same control over a fourteen-year-old that we do over a preschooler. And we don't expect the teenager to show love to us in the same way as a four-year-old. Both children are at very different places in their growth toward independence, and that demands a change in the way we mother each of these children.

I admit that many aspects of the "who am I?" question are intertwined. Let me give you another example from my childhood. When I was growing up, my mother constantly told me that the years of mothering young children were the best and happiest years of her life. The subtle message I got was that once those years were over, life was all downhill. So I felt I had to hold on fiercely to my children during those fleeting years, because once they began to need me less, life would be all downhill for me. I dreaded the thought of letting go. I dreaded the words *empty nest.*

In looking back, I think those were my mother's best years. She never again engaged in life with such vitality and enthusiasm as during those active mothering years, though deteriorating health contributed to her diminished activities. She never found other outlets that fulfilled her as much as her children, and she continued to depend upon us as adults for her main joys. She was not able to model a full life of interests beyond children.

I don't remember my mother talking about her vulnerabilities or the realities of her weaknesses as well as her strengths. Even as an adult, if I brought up a disagreement between us, she'd usually say, with parental authority and finality, "You just can't change me." End of discussion.

I know her resistance to change influenced me. I'm still learning that change is necessary and can be positive.

DO I STAGNATE IN MY NEED TO BE NEEDED?

Judith Viorst knows that motherly delight of feeling needed:

I was for a while—the One and Only Indispensable Mommy. The mommy who put on Band-Aids ... The mommy in "I want Mommy." ... And while all of that need and dependence were often encroaching and sometimes oppressive, there were, in exchange, some exceedingly sweet payoffs. As a friend of mine observed, "My son was

the only one in my life who squealed with delight whenever I entered a room."

Why wouldn't we miss that![5]

As our children grow up, we recognize, with a mixture of
pride and regret, that they need us less. One day one of our children came home from school obviously rankled about something.
After downing a peanut butter sandwich and milk in silence, he
confessed, "Something happened today at school, but I don't
want to tell you about it. It wasn't bad. It just hurt my feelings.
It's okay though. I've already prayed about it."

Proud? Yes.

Curious? Certainly!

But a bit sad that I wasn't needed as much? You bet.

We all need to be needed. That's healthy, normal human
behavior. Some of the need is obviously fulfilled by our children.
But the question is how that need is fulfilled and for how long.
Erik Erickson distinguishes between healthy and unhealthy fulfillment of that need, using the terms *generativity* as opposed to
stagnation. Generativity, defined in terms of "establishing and
guiding the next generation," is positive and life affirming. Stagnation, defined in terms of "personal impoverishment," results
when we fail to invest in concerns beyond ourselves.[6]

As our children grow up, our need to be needed by them must
be balanced with other areas of fulfillment in our lives.

DOES LOVE GET CONFUSED WITH NEED?

Soon after the sudden death of her husband Peter Marshall,
Catherine Marshall described the challenge of mothering her
nine-year-old:

The highest function of my mother love would be fulfilled
when my love was strong enough to cut the apron strings
and let my adult child move off into his own life. I would
succeed as a mother only when I had so reared my child

that he would no longer have need of me. Yet this is not tragedy; it is growth. This is no betrayal of love. This is love.[7]

Love and need. It's easy to wind the two around each other.

Somewhere along the way, our love may develop into an abnormal need for our children. The dependency role subtly gets reversed; without even knowing it, we have grown dependent upon our children to fulfill a need in our lives.

We may "need" a child to hold a disintegrating marriage together, as a friend recently discovered. She had confided that her marriage was in trouble.

"Are your children more important to you than your husband?" I asked her.

"Why, yes," she answered without hesitation, assuming that would be every mother's answer. Eventually, through counseling she realized she was getting more emotional satisfaction from her children than from her husband and establishing a dangerous pattern of dependence upon them.

When they are little, our children may demand more attention than a spouse, but if they become more important and a source of greater fulfillment than a spouse, we are headed for trouble. By definition, parenting is a temporary job. Our children will come and go. A spouse, we trust, will stay.

Some parents become overly dependent on their children in the face of tragedy. One young mother said that after her mother's death in a car accident, she took her daughter out of preschool for the rest of the year so she could spend the days at home with her. "My reaction to the loss of my mother was to hold on tighter to my daughter."

A single parent may become emotionally dependent on a child as a companion or confidant to fill the void left by the spouse, or as a helper to do the chores a spouse would normally do. (And yet the child in a single-parent household may gain confidence and independence from the responsibilities he or she shoulders out of necessity.)

Do I "Become" My Children?

Am I my child? Sometimes that question doesn't have a clear answer. Everything that happens to them feels like it happens to us. She gets a shot; I feel the needle. She's not invited to a birthday party; I feel the rejection. As we meet their needs, they start meeting our needs, and the edges of our separateness grow fuzzy.

Or our children become our report cards. If my child looks good, I am a good mother (no matter how I look myself). If my child does well in school, I am good and successful (no matter how successful I am in any other aspect of my life).

Phyllis Theroux writes, "We hold our children up, like mirrors, and search the reflection for proof that we have not failed, ostensibly as parents, in reality as human beings. Hard on ourselves, we are often doubly hard on them, asking them to perform better than we can."[8]

Many parents depend on their children for their identity or significance. They encourage the children to become all that they themselves wish they had been or could be; they look to their children to fill in the spaces of a less than satisfying life.

David Elkind, in his book *The Hurried Child,* ventures that there is a strong connection between a parent's job dissatisfaction and a disproportionate concern with the offspring's success in sports.[9] A father may push his son to become the athlete he was or wishes he had been. A mother may push her daughter to achieve what she didn't.

With our identities wrapped up in theirs, we let their successes become our successes; their failures, our failures. We let ourselves think that our dreams for them should become their dreams for themselves.

Many parents, blind to the separateness of their children, see that three must forever remain as one. Fathers are convinced that they are cutting a trail for their children to follow. Parents insist that children will finish all of college, whether they want to or not. Parents are deeply hurt when their children join a denomination different from theirs, molding the future into some shape other than what they had envisioned.[10]

ARE MY CHILDREN MY EXCUSE OR DIVERSION?

Sometimes we depend on our children as an excuse not to do or be anything else. Obviously, there is a period in life when children are a legitimate excuse. I distinctly remember how I felt after the birth of each child. It was as if the world had stopped to allow me to be this baby's mother. No one expected me to do laundry, shopping, or cooking. Momentarily, my purpose in life was clearly defined: I was to nurture this newborn. (That singleness of purpose didn't last long. In fact, if I suffered a postpartum depression, it was because I realized I had to pick up the plow and head on down the field to tend all my other responsibilities.)

Yes, a woman with babies and toddlers at home has a legitimate reason not to do much else. She has little time or energy. But humorist Erma Bombeck described a more sobering view of one mother's feelings as the last of her litter marched off to school:

> My excuse for everything just got on that bus. My excuse for not dieting, not getting a full-time job, not cleaning house, not re-upholstering the furniture, not going back to school, not having order in my life, not cleaning the oven. It is the end of an era. Now what do I do for the next 20 years of my life?[11]

Some women put off that decision and have another baby. I know someone who has a twelve-year-old, a six-year-old, and a baby. I saw her recently, pushing a stroller. "I'm so wrapped up in this baby," she gushed, sweeping him up in her arms and covering his cheeks with kisses. I was glad for her, yet also a bit sorry because I knew that inevitably she would have to face the reality of life without a baby. Someday a baby would not be a diversion from facing other "who am I?" issues.

OTHER FACTORS

Is letting go more difficult or different for a mother, father, single parent, or Christian parent? As one counselor explained, what controls the level of difficulty is not so much the status as the emotional makeup of the person and the established pattern of the parent-child relationship. In other words, we can't stereotype the responses. But having said that, there are some general observations that might give a bit more insight into your parenting patterns, especially in terms of individual children.

Mothers and fathers may face the release of sons and daughters differently, because of the subtle ways men and women treat children differently. It's been said that fathers care about their children's success; mothers care more about their children's happiness. That's a big difference right there. But also, from the birth of a child all the way through the growing-up years, fatherhood generally requires fewer life changes than motherhood.

Though the culture is changing, mothers still assume many of the responsibilities of the dependent years of a child's life. Generally, a stay-at-home mother is emotionally more aware of her child's milestones of independence than a father is. A child's going off to school may not tug at a dad's heart because his schedule is not as changed by the milestone. Yet sometimes mothers are more prepared than fathers for the final release of children, because they gradually adjust through small steps along the way. Weaning, starting preschool, and finally all-day-long school give mothers a chance to let go slowly.

As for gender differences of children, some mothers may overprotect their sons and consequently have a harder time letting go and handing those responsibilities over to future daughters-in-law. But these same mothers may expect more out of their daughters as they grow up. "Up until we left home, my mother always asked my brother what he wanted for lunch and always expected me to fix my own lunch," one female college student said. Fathers, on the other hand, may overprotect their daughters and encourage their sons to be tough.

Single parents face a complicated set of dependence and independence issues. Sometimes unhealthy dependence results, and in other instances shared custody or weekend visits forces a single parent to practice letting go, both emotionally and physically.

Christian parents often have difficulty letting go, because they see such disparity between the values they teach and the realities their children face in the world beyond their doorsteps. The temptations are frightening, as are the consequences of unwise choices.

Personal Evaluation

In his book *Adolescent-Parental Separation,* clinical psychologist Michael Bloom describes parents who do and don't let go easily. Those who let go easily are self-confident, comfortable with change, good at interpersonal relationships, able to learn from their adolescents, and able to satisfy their own needs as well as their children's. They also value independence and autonomy for themselves and their children, have a clear sense of personal values, and see the separation process as a natural part of growth.

Parents who have difficulty letting go don't deal with change easily, lack clarity about values and identity, are uneasy about communicating differences with others, and view the separation process as desertion by their children.[12] Looking at these issues and patterns can be difficult. Since becoming a mother, I've thought about the vulnerabilities that affect my ability and willingness to let go. I entered motherhood with some high (and unrealistic) expectations and a few nagging Mommy Fears. Mostly, I

> *Parents who let go easily are self-confident, comfortable with change, and able to satisfy their own needs.*

assumed I'd do a good job of loving my children and that the role would bring out the best in me. Obviously, I faced some reality checks, which caused me to search my childhood and examine what makes me who I am today, and how that affects my parenting.

However, as I assessed how I was mothered, I cringed a bit, knowing I have unwittingly done some of the same things my mother did, and surely my children will engage in the same assessment of me. And why not? I know in my head, even if I don't feel it in my heart, that these are healthy assessments, and I would be most flattered if they come to the conclusion that I have been a "good-enough mother," as described by Dr. Henry Cloud and Dr. John Townsend in *The Mom Factor:*

> Good-enough moms are aware of their weaknesses and tendencies. They are working on doing the right thing for themselves and their child. They are getting help in their mothering weaknesses from safe people.
>
> Good-enough moms assume they will make mistakes with their child, and they factor that in to their mothering. They know they won't always be there as they should. They aren't surprised by their failures; they are prepared to correct them, learn from them, and move on.[13]

In fact, the best thing we can do when we recognize our mistakes is admit them to our children. If they see us acknowledging our weaknesses as well as our strengths and desiring growth and change, they will be quicker to do the same. Regardless of our age differences, we have something in common with our children: we are flawed and imperfect people with strengths and weaknesses. When we recognize this and forgive each other for the less-than-perfect parts of ourselves, we are loving the way God calls us to love.

God has a purpose in all of this. Recognizing our imperfections helps us know our need for him. And in knowing that need and accepting him, we receive his grace and forgiveness, which gives us the freedom to be more vulnerable and real, to admit our imperfections to ourselves and others. This is called humility or brokenness, and with it we enter God's divine and seamless cycle of receiving and giving his love, which is the safest place to be, especially for moms.

PERSONAL COMMANDMENTS

Following a personal assessment of the factors that affect our parenting, especially those that influence our ability to let go, it's helpful to come up with personal guidelines that remind us of our vulnerabilities. At least then we can say, "Oops . . . there I go again." Here are some of my own do's and don'ts from my early years of mothering.

MY PERSONAL DO'S

• *Do trust in God.* Always. God was not a regular part of my childhood, but I am choosing to live differently. Nothing in life has made me more aware of my need for God than my mothering. I can't be loving and patient and kind and wise without God. I can't face all the unknowns without trusting him. I can't live with my mistakes without his forgiveness. I am totally dependent upon him, so praying and reading my Bible need to be regular parts of my life.

• *Do put my marriage first.* Children change a marriage, so this is a difficult if not seemingly impossible goal, especially when children are young. But it is a heart attitude lived out by my actions. It is based on a commitment to continually seek intimacy, which is not only about sex but also about choosing to be kind to each other and to work at understanding each other, especially as we both grow and change. Children change a marriage. Without this commitment, couples can slowly grow apart as they raise their children and find themselves as strangers when the children leave home.

• *Do invest in areas of interest outside of my children.* My role as a mother can consume me, so I need to balance my investment in my children with other interests that develop who I am as an individual, apart from mothering. Moms need to remember the dreams we had before we became moms and keep rekindling our potential and individuality.

• *Do check my motives.* Sometimes I am tempted to make choices that meet my needs rather than my children's needs. Of course, at times that's necessary. If I have to get to a doctor's appointment and a toddler is dawdling, insisting on dressing himself, I have to meet my need to hurry rather than his need to exercise independence. But I have to remember that, in general, I am here for my children; they are not here for me. And when I am faced with a choice or decision, I have to ask myself, "Am I doing this for their good, or for my good? Am I meeting their need, or mine? Am I doing this because I need to be right, or because it is the right thing to do?" Raising children is about meeting their need to grow toward independence, not my need for fulfillment.

• *Do check my priorities.* Because the child-rearing season of life passes quickly, I need to take advantage of it by cutting some of the stress and busyness out of my life. I have to determine what the main thing is, and then keep the main thing the main thing. These questions help me determine my priorities:

What am I doing now that no one else can do?
(high priority)

What am I doing now that someone else can do?
(low priority)

What am I doing now that will matter in five years?
(high priority)

My Personal Don'ts

• *Don't fight my children's battles.* I know myself well enough to know that this is a temptation. People can hurt me, but they better not mess with my kids. I'm instinctively protective. When someone hurts my children's feelings or treats them unfairly, I feel like a mother bear; I have to control the snarl growing in my throat. Though children sometimes need their parents to be their advocates, we need to teach them to defend or explain themselves with appropriate words.

• *Don't try to make life fair.* I remember that as a child, when faced with one of life's little injustices, I would wail to my mother, "But that's not fair!" And she would always answer, "Life isn't fair, dear." It used to make me so mad, because I wanted life to be fair. Our own children echo that same pitiful cry, and I'm always torn between wanting to make life fair for them and making them strong enough to cope with all the inevitable unfairness they will face in life. If I overprotect them, I rob them of the opportunity to grow through suffering.

• *Don't manipulate by guilt.* I never liked being sent on guilt trips as a child, and I know my children don't like it, so I vow not to lay a guilt trip on them. But sometimes it happens anyway. I ask my son to dump the kitchen garbage. He is watching TV and says, "As soon as this program is over." That's not the answer I want. "I guess I'll just have to do it," I say, and I start banging the trash can around. My words and actions are intended to make him feel guilty so he'll get up and dump the garbage for me. Manipulation by guilt is a dishonest indirect way to make somebody do something. "Derek, I need you to dump the garbage before dinner" is more honest.

• *Don't assume responsibility for my children's problems.* I'm a Fix-It Mom, and I like to solve my children's problems. For instance, a child asks, "Where is my shoe?" so I begin looking for it. But I notice the oddest thing. The shoe owner then stops looking because I have assumed responsibility for this problem.

• *Don't let my children be my report card.* No question about it, in our world we are judged by what we produce, so it's easy to fall into the trap of letting our children become our report card. We put bumper stickers on our cars that identify us as the parent of a Fairview Honor Roll Student. We proudly wear a sweatshirt with our child's college logo on it, especially if that school is known and recognized. Our children's success becomes acknowledgment that we are good parents. I vow not to let my ego get tangled up with my children's accomplishments, but it's a temptation.

Who we are as individuals makes a great difference in the way we embrace or resist the challenge of loving and letting go. Though we are constantly growing and changing, it's helpful to take a look at ourselves and consider the ways we might encourage or discourage our children's growth toward independence. We also realize along the way that though we are helping our children grow up, they are helping us grow up too.

FOR REFLECTION

1. Consider your childhood. How did your parents encourage your independence? How did they discourage it?

2. How will you parent differently from the way you were parented? What will you try to duplicate?

3. What are some personality characteristics that may affect your ability to let go?

4. Identify two personal do's and two don'ts.

PONDERPOINT

LETTING GO IS ...

To let go doesn't mean to stop caring,
It means I can't do it for someone else.
To let go is not to enable,

But to allow learning from natural consequences.
To let go is to admit powerlessness,
Which means the outcome is not in my hands.
To let go is not to try to change or blame another,
I can only change myself.
To let go is not to care for, but to care about.
To let go is not to fix, but to be supportive.
To let go is not to judge, but to allow another to
   be a human being.
To let go is not to be in the middle of arranging
   all the outcomes,
But to allow others to effect their own outcomes.
To let go is not to be protective,
It is to permit another to face reality.
To let go is not to deny, but to accept.
To let go is not to nag, scold, or argue,
But to search out my own shortcomings and to
   correct them.
To let go is not to regret the past,
But to grow and live for the future.
To let go is to fear less and love more.

ANONYMOUS

6

Building a Firm Foundation

Blessed is the family where growing children are allowed to become what God would have them become as soon as possible, and blessed are the parents who encourage that to happen and, as fast as they can, get out of the way.

CHARLES SWINDOLL, "RELEASING THE REINS"

I see a hidden assumption in this insightful "beatitude" for parents by Charles Swindoll. When these parents "get out of the way," their children's lives won't come crashing down, because those parents have helped to build their children's lives upon a firm foundation.

A firm foundation is critical to the stability of a structure. It strengthens both from the ground up and the inside out.

When building a good house, foundations start with a plan, a well-thought-out blueprint that is the result of hard work, tough questions, and dreams about what the house should look like. When building a family where children are raised and launched, the same kind of plan or blueprint is important. But where does one start?

A family mission statement is a good beginning because it sums up the goals and purpose of your family. It both underlies and overarches your growing family. It is a big-picture statement that keeps you on track and gives direction to your choices. It guides and strengthens. Though adults may mosey along quite contentedly without clarifying their values, once they face the task of raising children, it becomes important to identify what matters to their family. Although the task of coming up with such a statement may sound daunting, it can grow quite easily out of a lively brainstorming session that starts with questions like these:

> *Once we face the responsibility of raising children, we're suddenly forced to look at what we stand for as a family.*

- What makes our family unique?
- What do we stand for?
- What do we value?
- What are our passions?
- What is the goal of our parenting?
- What values do we hope to pass on to our children, which we hope they will pass on to their children?
- What character traits would we like our children to have?
- What would we like our family to look like in five years . . . ten years . . . twenty years?

Here are two examples of family mission statements from the parents of young children:

Our goal is to live in harmony by considering each other's needs as more important than our own.

Our purpose as a family is to provide a safe environment for children and grown-ups alike to learn more about loving and serving Jesus through the act of learning how to love and serve each other.[1]

As you can see, family mission statements give only general direction to the structure of the family. With a mission statement, you can more easily identify the specific building blocks of your family's foundation. Some of the questions on the previous page may guide your thinking.

For instance, the question, "What makes this family unique?" helps you think about qualities that set your family apart from other families and give your children an important sense of belonging. Likes and dislikes may unify your family. Shared traditions, patterns of speech, and systems of operations make a family unit function and provide blocks for its foundation:

- At our house we always pray before we eat.
- At our house we get five dollars a week for allowance, but we buy our own school lunches.
- At our house we always have doughnuts on Saturday mornings.
- At our house we celebrate family birthdays with balloons and presents at breakfast.

Each family has a system for disposing of newspapers and aluminum cans and has rules about the television, the telephone, and bed making. These may be insignificant rules or systems by themselves, but the knowledge of them causes the feeling of belonging in a family and establishes a bonding loyalty among members—part of the foundation we lay for our children.

BUILDING BLOCKS OF A FIRM FOUNDATION

Jesus talked about the wise man who built his house on rock. "The rain came down, the streams rose, and the winds blew and beat against that house; yet it did not fall, because it had its foundation on the rock" (Matt. 7:25). Not so for the foolish man who built his house on sand; the same ravages assaulted his less secure house, and "it fell with a great crash" (Matt. 7:27).

If we want our children to become strong, we must build into them the potential for strength. We must give them early in life a firm foundation of values upon which all future knowledge, abilities, and behavior will be built. They will draw strength from this foundation when facing temptations, assaults, and challenges.

Another analogy is the core theory, which likens kids to apples and onions. An apple has a core: the tough, fibrous, seedy center that remains even if the skin is bruised or torn away. An onion, on the other hand, has no core. When an onion is peeled away, nothing remains. God wants us to plant the seeds of Christian values deep within our children's tender souls when they are young and pliable. Kids with seed cores may be bruised or torn on the outside by life's experiences. But no matter how many mistakes they make, they will eventually get back on track because their core—their values system—remains intact.

If our kids develop a core of good values early in life and do well up through sixth grade, no matter how rebellious or difficult they become in adolescence, eventually they will emerge again as good kids. Their core will carry them through. Their values give them structure and strength to withstand the harsh circumstances of life.

Surely God wants us to give our children Christian values, which are the critical building blocks of a firm foundation— grace, compassion, loyalty, commitment, integrity, perseverance, humility, and kindness, to name a few. So our first step as parents is to identify those values. Our children's values will shape their attitudes and therefore their behavior for life. They will affect the way our children view God, self, and others; our children's attitudes in these three key areas grow out of their understanding of those values of grace, compassion, loyalty, and commitment that are learned, primarily, in their family relationships. That's where the building blocks are put in place.

How do we put these critical blocks in place? Probably you are familiar with the acronym TLC, which stands for tender loving care. Just change the last letter, and you can remember a new acronym for building these values into the hearts of your children: TLM—through teaching, loving, and modeling.

BUILDING VALUES THROUGH TEACHING

We are our children's first and most important teachers. We give them instruction and information; we use examples; we tell stories; we sing and read to them. Our children are like sponges, absorbing what they hear and see, especially when they are young. That's why our influence on them is so critically important when their foundations are under construction and their minds are so able to absorb what we teach them.

Teaching our children begins with very basic Christian and family principles that undergird the foundation for family rules: God made families because he believes they are important. He put the first four people—Adam and Eve, and their sons Cain and Abel—into a family. God knew this first family, and all families, would face struggles, so he gave them rules to live by, rules he also wants us to live by today. He tells parents to love their children and to teach them to obey; he tells children to obey their parents.

When our children were toddlers, Lynn told them we have three rules in our house that come from Scripture. The number one rule is "Never tell a lie." The number two rule is "Think of others." The number three rule is "Don't forget where you came from," which means stick together and help one another. Over the years, we did not simply tell the children our family rules; we also taught them how to apply those rules.

In *Building Character*, Dr. Kay Kuzma lists thirteen qualities she wants her children to develop: faithfulness, orderliness, self-discipline, happiness, perseverance, honesty, thoughtfulness, efficiency, responsibility, respect, enthusiasm, humility and peacefulness. She works toward this goal by emphasizing one of these qualities a week, going through each of them four times every year.[2]

Children have an incredible capacity for memorization. Our children sing countless popular tunes or repeat television commercials verbatim. Repetition enables them to memorize, and memorization, especially of Scripture, is a powerful teaching tool. "I can do all things through Christ who strengthens me," one youngster tells himself on the starting block in his first swim meet. "The Lord is my strength and my shield; in him my heart trusts," a child repeats to herself as she starts a new school year.

Author Elisabeth Elliot claims, "I was raised on Scripture the way some kids are raised on vitamins." To help imprint God's Word and principles on my children's memory, I kept a supply of three-by-five cards and a pad of sticky notes handy; I'd jot down appropriate Scripture or inspirational sayings to post, especially for the refrigerator door. Some families use a similar card system to memorize a verse a week, repeating it and talking about it at mealtime. Christian bookstores sell simple card systems that promote Scripture memorization.

The spiritual foundation we give our children early in life will become the basis of their own personal faith, so we build God's truth into their hearts, by teaching them about Jesus and his promises, and making him real in their lives.

And these words which I command you this day shall be upon your heart; and you shall teach them diligently to your children, and shall talk of them when you sit in your house, and when you walk by the way, and when you lie down, and when you rise.

Deuteronomy 6:6–7 RSV

I used to think "diligently" meant I had to dance around every sunbeam in the living room, proclaiming the goodness of every object in sight because God made it. I used to think "talking" meant reciting Scripture all day long. But if we do that, we'll soon lose credibility with our children. Larry Christenson translates this Scripture to mean "a quiet threading of God's Word through the warp and woof of family life."[3] I like that interpretation because it tells us to be real and relevant when weaving God's truth into the fabric of our everyday lives.

As parents we can take any experience and use it to teach our children principles of faithful living. I remember one particularly vivid experience with Lindsay. She was eight years old and just learning to ski. At the end of her first day of lessons, she wanted to show me what she'd learned, so I took her up the chairlift for the last run of the day. We headed for a beginners' slope, plainly marked by large green signs. But somehow I took the wrong cut-off. Next thing I knew, we were in the middle of an expert slope with nowhere to go but down.

We teetered on the brink of what looked like a cliff, carved by treacherously deep moguls. Only a mother and novice skier like me would understand the sheer terror I felt at that moment. "I can't do this, Mom," Lindsay stated in a quiet voice. That was an understatement. I knew she couldn't do it, and I seriously doubted I could do it.

The slope was deserted. I wasn't surprised. *Who would take a slope like this on purpose?* I wondered. "Let's pray, Lindsay," I said automatically, because I was helpless.

Pray we did, and within seconds two ski patrolmen schussed into sight above us. They could read the panic in my body language. "Need any help?" one asked.

Our problem was no problem to them. One took Lindsay's poles; the other simply put her small form between his legs, held on to her, and expertly threaded his way down through the valley of moguls to the bottom of the hill. The grace of God got me down behind them, and the experience gave me a chance to tell Lindsay that I don't believe in coincidences or good luck and that God sent those ski patrolmen to us in answer to prayer. It was a powerful teachable moment, and we still remember the day God sent us two angels in ski patrol outfits. It was a day the living God was real in our lives.

BUILDING VALUES THROUGH LOVING

By the way we love them, we build into the hearts of our children values and attitudes about God, self, and others. From the day they come into our lives, our children absorb our love. An infant's first developmental need is for bonding and attatchment, which is met through our comforting, touching, talking, and cuddling. A child's sense of security and trust is established within the first few months of life; the nurturing sense of love is as critical to their future as good nutrition.

Our relationship with our children models the relationship we have with our heavenly Father. Our love should be as much like his love as humanly possible: unconditional, consistent, and full of grace. Our children need to understand that they don't earn our love, just as we don't earn God's love. Our love for them is not based on their performance, which is a relief, because children perform badly at times. At least ours have. They spilled their milk at restaurants, shared family secrets with strangers, and broke things "by accident." They fought with each other in church. They embarrassed and disappointed me, but I hope they knew I loved them even when I didn't like what they did.

I assume they knew that, but I was repeatedly surprised to see how much they liked to hear my assurance: "There is nothing you can say or do that will ever change my love for you. I may be disappointed, angry, or hurt, but I will never, never love you less." This is a message our children will believe if it is repeated in actions and words, and it is a message that will help them understand God's grace and forgiving love.

Our love is expressed in many ways. It is both tough and tender. Sometimes it is hugs and kisses. Other times it is discipline and setting limits. But usually it is a combination of both.

UNIQUE LOVE

Love understands the individual needs of individual children. God has created each person, each child, uniquely. Comments like, "He acts just like you," or, "She sounds just like you," some-

> *Love understands the individual needs of individual children.*

times make Lynn or me feel good, but I feel even better when I see things that Lynn and I can't claim at all: watching a six-year-old with chubby little hands patiently finger-training her parakeet (when I have no such patience); watching an eight-year-old ride a horse with grace and assurance (when her father and I are nonequestrian); seeing a ten-year-old with the self-discipline to give up sugar (when I lack such willpower). I am in awe of how God has created them uniquely—each different from the other and from us, the parents.

Some parents claim they can feel the differences in their children even during pregnancy. One kicks; the other is quiet. One responds to movement and activity; another doesn't. One arrives on time; the other is two weeks late.

It didn't take us long to recognize the differences in our first two children. One had trouble falling asleep. The other slept easily and soundly. The same pattern was evident ten—and twenty—years later.

In part, some of these traits may be due to the way parents handle first and second children, but much, I am convinced, is due to their God-given bents. Proverbs 22:6 tells us to "Train up a child in the way he should go and in keeping with his individual gift or bent" (AMPLIFIED). Bents are not learned, automatically inherited, or shaped by the environment. Bents are God-given, inborn characteristics.

Larry Christenson notes, "We are to train up the child not simply in the way that any and every child should go, but also in the [specific and unique] way in which he should go."⁴We are to train our children according to the unique personality God has given them, which is definitely not *exactly* like ours, or may not be exactly as we would choose for them.

How can parents recognize their children's bents? It takes various elements of love: time, intentionality, and sensitivity. We need to use our senses: observing, listening, talking.

In a book titled "Every Child Has a Gift," teacher Hughes Mearns advises parents to discover their children's gifts through observation. Observe them when they are off guard, he suggests. Watch them at picnics, on the playground, during a game, or quietly at home. Observe them without judgment, as if they were someone else's children. Stop trying to make them what they ought to be; rather, see what they are now. Listen to them; encourage them to express their opinions at the dinner table or before bedtime.⁵ When I registered each child in preschool, I had to fill out a detailed questionnaire. What is your child's favorite activity? What are her fears? What makes him sad? What makes her happy? What is his favorite color, book, and TV character? The questions made me uneasy because I didn't know all the answers. But they also reminded me of my responsibility to get to know our kids.

To get to know each child, share observations with teachers, coaches, friends, other parents, and especially spouses. At different ages, playing board games can be a means of discerning differences, likes, and dislikes.

Spend time, planned or unplanned, alone with each child. This allows you to get to know him or her and also helps encourage your own respect for the child's separateness and individuality. This is especially important with children close in age. One mother said, "We had two children a year apart, and I found myself lumping the two of them together more than our other two, who were born six years later and separated by four years."

To give children time alone, one father alternates taking each child on out-of-town business trips when his schedule permits. One mother takes a different child to lunch once a week. I especially relish time alone in the car with a single child. For a few moments, we are each other's captive audience.

Some differences in children are due to God-given bents. Some may be due to the inevitable changes in parental love as the family matures. Do you identify with any of these stereotypes? Traditionally, firstborn children who receive their parents' undivided attention are conservative and conforming. Because their parents have high expectations of them, they tend to be overachievers and perfectionists. Second or middle children tend to be friendlier and less demanding. They are diplomatic and skilled at compromising. On the other hand, parents often are more reluctant to allow the baby or last child the freedom to grow up. Yet these children are usually charming, happy, and fun loving, because they have been showered with affection.

A healthy, unique parental love does well not to compare one child with another or expect one to be just like a brother or sister. A family's black sheep may simply feel he or she can't live up to the standards set by siblings or expected by parents. Children with different bents will bring home different grades on their report cards. Lynn and I read our children's report cards alone with each child instead of making the review a family affair.

How does respect for the uniqueness of each child influence the way you show your love to that child? How does your love respect each child's uniqueness? The strong-willed child? The compliant child? Those two personalities respond to rules and discipline very differently. And then there's differences in age. For example, a child's age probably will determine the appropriate bedtime.

What is fair in love? When it comes to rules, we have a challenge treating children differently, because they have such keen memories. They remember exactly how old Derek was "when you let him go out on a date"! It's as if they think a pattern was cast in concrete with the first child. We try to be fair with our children, but that doesn't mean we treat them exactly the same. Or maybe the rules are the same, but we enforce them differently according to each child's need and ability to accept responsibility.

Our efforts to be fair also cause them to expect fairness, and we all know that life isn't fair. If I buy Lindsay a pair of shoes, do I feel I should buy Kendall a pair, even though Kendall doesn't need shoes? Do I keep track of Christmas presents to make sure each child gets the same number? If they see me counting up this way, surely they will count too, expecting life to be fair.

Our challenge is to deal with differences in children's bents, temperaments, and ages with sensitivity, to build their self-esteem and confidence, and to equip them to reach their maximum potential. How can you focus on a child's strengths, not weaknesses? How can you make each feel good about the person he or she was made to be by the Creator, the Architect, the Master Planner of their souls?

Kids continually ask themselves, "Am I okay?" They need our loving affirmation, because what they think of themselves is based on how they think others see them. Especially when they are young, we are the mirrors that reflect their sense of self, and they need our positive encouragement.

Answering the question, "What do your kids really want?" Phyllis Theroux writes, "I think it is to feel that they are good—deep down, where maybe no one else, including themselves, can see it."[6] That is not only what they want most; it is what they need most.

TOUGH LOVE

Sometimes we must exercise tough love, which means giving up a short-term benefit in hopes of reaching a long-term, better goal. It means teaching children to be accountable and accept the consequences of their actions. We sacrifice the comfort of pleasing our children at the moment in an effort to help them learn an important life lesson. We do what we sense will be good for them in the long run.

We say no to the three-year-old who whines for cookies before dinner. We help an older child understand the meaning of commitment and the importance of finishing the soccer season even though quitting would feel good right now.

Sometimes midway through a session of lessons or a season of soccer, a child knows and you know this activity is not his or her bent. In our home, because of the commitment made, the child had to remain in the program for the duration of the session, though of course that duration was sometimes nebulous. Take piano lessons, for example. At age nine, Lindsay begged to start piano lessons. We agreed. About a year later, she tired of the tedious practice time and wanted to quit and take flute in the school band. We felt she should stick with the piano lessons long enough to get some lasting benefit from her investment of time and our investment of money. So we compromised. We didn't set a time frame, but we set a certain level of accomplishment as a goal. She had to reach the end of a certain book before she could quit. That gave her a goal and incentive. Music is not her bent, so we didn't continue to force her. But we tried to help her make the most of the experience.

When Derek was diagnosed with diabetes, his doctor encouraged us to send him away to a weeklong camp for diabetics, where he would meet other children who shared his problem, learn more about diabetes control, and gain confidence in his ability to take care of himself. At age nine, he did not want to go. But we gently and firmly insisted, because we believed the experience would help him take an important step toward independence.

The night before he was to leave, we were in his room, stuffing clothes into his duffel bag. He sat down on his bed, and his voice began to quiver. "I know you can't change it now, but why are you making me go?" he asked with tears in his eyes.

We'd been through the reasons a hundred times, and my heart was breaking for him as he anticipated the homesickness. It would have been so easy to call the whole thing off at that moment; it would be so difficult to leave him at the camp in the morning.

"When you walk away," he stammered, trying to control himself, "I will feel terrible." I prayed that night and the next day for angels to surround Derek and for strength for me to walk away.

The sun was bright that June morning when we left the suddenly small, brave figure on the steps of a rickety camp cabin. With a quick hug, I turned and took a long walk away. I endured a week that was almost as hard on me as it was on him. That was tough love.

We look back now and know the experience was good for Derek. In fact, I believe camp experiences beginning in late elementary school are good for all children, because they learn they can cope away from home. Children should not face that challenge for the first time as a college freshman.

Parenting with tough love means setting limits. Children need limits. Setting limits not only protects them but teaches them self-control and self-discipline. But those lessons aren't learned if limits are not maintained through discipline. In fact, the Bible is filled with verses about the rewards of discipline and the parent's responsibility to discipline a child in love.

Talking about the Christian life in general, Hebrews 12:11 says, "No discipline seems pleasant at the time, but painful. Later on, however, it produces a harvest of righteousness and peace for those who have been trained by it."

Setting and maintaining limits gives children a sense of security and creates a predictable environment where they can meet new challenges confidently. Proper discipline rewards and reinforces good behavior and discourages bad behavior. It develops the conscience, which teaches children to respond to right and wrong, even when parents are not around.

Let's look at three characteristics of limits and discipline that teach our children virtue.

Discipline Should Be Firm

We say what we mean and mean what we say. Too often, I get impatient or frustrated and threaten a child with consequences I know—and the child knows—I can't or won't carry out. Before a family outing, one child keeps teasing another child. "Stop bugging your sister, or you won't go with us," I tell him. I don't mean that. He has to go with us. I don't have a baby-sitter, and I'm not willing to stay home with him. We lose our effectiveness if we say what we don't mean.

The same principle applies to nagging. I call nagging "nonsense without a consequence." It is telling someone something he or she already knows. Usually over and over again. The kids tune me out when I keep repeating something. The first time a request or directive is made, it is informational. After that, it becomes nagging. The limits and consequences should be clear from the start.

Discipline Should Be Fair

The Bible twice commands parents to be fair in disciplining their children: "Fathers, do not provoke your children to anger, but bring them up in the discipline and instruction of the Lord" (Eph. 6:4 RSV) and "Fathers, do not provoke your children, lest they become discouraged" (Col. 3:21 RSV). The punishment has to fit the infraction. A first-time offense does not bring the same consequence as a repeat offense. An offense committed accidentally does not bring the same consequence as one committed on purpose. A child dropping a plate does not get the same punishment as a child purposely throwing the plate to the floor.

Discipline Should Be Consistent

If a consequence for problem behavior is identified and communicated, that consequence should be carried out consistently.

"If you hit your sister, you will have to go to your room for half an hour." Once that consequence is stated, we have to follow through with it consistently, even when Grandma and Grandpa and two cousins are visiting. Consistent enforcement helps children connect actions with consequences and helps them make good choices. The connection between choices and consequences prepares them for life in the real world.

In the real world, if Dad gets caught driving fifty miles per hour in a thirty-miles-per-hour zone, he gets a ticket. If Mom is on a diet but nibbles cookies all day, she will gain instead of lose weight. If the electric bill is not paid, the electric company may turn the electricity off.

We have a responsibility to run our homes as much like the real world as possible. The consequences of misbehavior or poor choices must be fair—logical and age appropriate—and consistently enforced.

BUILDING VALUES THROUGH MODELING

We transmit values to our children by the way we live. To use the familiar phrase, "Values are caught more than taught." What we do speaks louder than what we say, and our children do as they see done. Observe how they mimic us: the phrases they use, the tone of voice in talking to friends or siblings. Even their bad habits are often our bad habits.

I remember a memorable antismoking television commercial sponsored by the American Heart Association, a commercial with no words but a dramatic message. It opens with a little boy and his daddy walking through the woods together on a sunny day. The boy keeps looking up at his father adoringly, trying to imitate his every move. The little guy adjusts his identical hat to the same cockeyed angle, stuffs his fists in his pockets, and throws stones into a pond, just like Daddy. Finally the two sit down together under a tree, the boy still watching his father intently. Just then Dad pulls out a pack of cigarettes, lights one up, leans back, and tosses the pack down in the grass beside his son. The boy looks down at the cigarettes, then looks back up and smiles at his daddy, hero worship still in his eyes.

"A Child Learns What He Lives" is the title of a familiar inspirational poem often seen hanging in pediatricians' offices and homes. It begins, "If a child lives with criticism, he learns to condemn. If a child lives with hostility, he learns to fight." It ends with "If a child lives with security, he learns to have faith. If a child lives with approval, he learns to like himself. If a child lives with acceptance and friendship, he learns to find love in the world."

Whether or not we like it or even know it, we teach by example every day of our lives; and our children learn by watching. How do they see us treating a waitress? What kind of sportsmanship do they see in us at sporting events? Like me, I'm sure you've seen parents shout at the referees, coaches, and even their own children. In our community, the soccer league responded to this behavior with a "Parents' Code of Conduct" that reads:

> Children have more need of example than criticism: Attempt to relieve the pressure of competition, not increase it; do not openly question an official's judgment and honesty. Officials are symbols of fair play, integrity and sportsmanship: Accept the results of each game by encouraging your child to be gracious in victory and to turn defeat into victory by working toward improvement.

Modeling is a continual challenge for most of us. We make mistakes. We lose our patience and say things we shouldn't. But if we admit these mistakes to our children, we model humility and brokenness and truth—that God loves and works through less-than-perfect people.

In her small book *If My Kids Drive Me Crazy, Am I a Bad Mom?* Janet Chester Bly advises mothers to "remember that you're only human. Some days you'll respond to your kids brilliantly; other days you'll make mistakes. Learning from those mistakes and saying you're sorry are what count, both for you and for your children. Kids are resilient. They also know when, beneath it all, you really love them."[7]

ATTITUDES BUILT ON SOLID VALUES

A building is shaped by the foundation on which it is built. Similarly, the family values transmitted by teaching, loving, and modeling shape our children's attitudes about God, self, and others. As you look at your own family's mission, values, and priorities, consider how you are influencing your children's attitudes in these three areas.

> *The family values transmitted by teaching, loving, and modeling shape our children's attitudes about God, self, and others.*

GOD

What do we want our children to know about God? The answer to this question is foundational to their spiritual growth and life. God is always present, always loving, always forgiving, and always in control when we turn to him and trust him. The footings of these foundational truths are put into place in their lives as early as we know to teach them.

One of my regrets is that I did not receive these footings as a child. Except for a few psalms, the memories of some Easter sunrise services, and grace before dinner on Thanksgiving, I didn't have much teaching about Jesus. It's as if I had to do some reconstructing of the foundation of my life as I learned about Jesus in high school and beyond. That's when God became my security in the midst of my moodiness and confusion about the world around me. That's when I felt a growing sense of God's presence within the core of my being.

The words of this simple children's song sum up the truth that children need to learn: "Jesus loves me, this I know, for the Bible tells me so. Little ones to him belong; they are weak, but he is strong." The profound truth of these words will ground children in the reality and security of God's presence and love. Their childlike faith is built upon that solid foundation. Upon that truth, they learn about God's unconditional love, grace, and forgiveness, concepts that are experienced before they are put into words.

SELF

In a healthy family a child gains a healthy sense of self: realizing that he or she is a unique individual who is separate and different from a parent and siblings and loved by God and parents. On the basis of this knowledge, the child builds a crucially important sense of self-worth, confidence, and the ability to be comfortable with who he or she is, which includes recognizing he or she is not ideal or perfect. This healthy concept of self gives a child a sense of security; it leads to self-control, the ability to make good choices and set personal boundaries. Learning to accept and love oneself precedes learning to love others.

OTHERS

We live in relationship with others, so our children's attitudes about others is crucial to their growth and development. Treating others with compassion and kindness grows out of their understanding that this world is not "all about me," which goes against their natural tendency to be self-focused. It grows out of learning respect, which teaches that the world does not belong to them only and that they have to learn to recognize and honor the needs of others. It is built on the Golden Rule: Do unto others as you would have others do unto you.

WRAP-UP

As our children grow, we loosen, not tighten, the reins. If we reverse this order and are permissive when they are young and then tighten our control as they grow and seek independence, we are in for a tough time. So are they. Parents who inconsistently enforce the rules with their preschoolers will have a hard time insisting their sixteen-year-old be home by midnight.

FOR REFLECTION

1. This meaningful exercise can help you identify the values you will try to pass on to your children: Imagine attending your own funeral. What would family members say about you? Are you satisfied with those remarks? If not, what would you like to change?

2. Name five of your values. Identify one way you will pass each of these values on to your children.

3. A family mission statement completes this sentence: "The purpose of our family is to _____." (Example: learn to love God and others.) Complete the sentence for your family.

4. The acronym TLM stands for teaching, loving, modeling— the ways we build values into our children. Which is easiest for you and why? Which is most difficult and why?

PONDERPOINT

TWENTY-ONE PRACTICAL PARENTING TIPS

1. Let them know you love them, no matter what.
2. Help them find something they feel good about being good at.
3. Keep rules to a minimum. Keep the main thing the main thing.

4. Loosen, don't tighten, the reins as they grow.
5. Let them be kids. Don't expect them to act like adults.
6. Encourage them to pursue their dreams, not your expectations.
7. Don't nag.
8. Teach them how to think, not what to think.
9. Allow them to make choices and experience the consequences of those choices.
10. Enlarge their circles and allow others to fill in the spaces you can't always fill.
11. Don't regularly do for them what they can do for themselves.
12. Don't fight their battles or try to make life fair.
13. Treat them with respect. Let them have and voice their own opinions.
14. Don't give them your worries.
15. Lighten up. Have fun together.
16. Be real. Admit your mistakes. Apologize.
17. Find common ground.
18. Make the most of life's irretrievable moments.
19. Get a life . . . your own life.
20. Pray for them. Unceasingly.
21. Trust God.

Remember, it is *never* too late to make an eternal difference in the lives of your children. Start where you are . . . today.

7

Early Training Rules

A good mother is like a quilt. She keeps her children
warm but doesn't smother them.

ANONYMOUS

Before our first child was born, Lynn and I promised each other that having a baby would not change us. We watched how becoming parents had changed some of our friends. They began acting all goofy, talking baby talk in high-pitched voices and assuming that topics like the color of their baby's stools was actually interesting to other people. Then they'd do absolutely disgusting things like stick their fingers in their baby's diapers just to see if something was in there. They always acted like their baby was the best baby in the whole world, and their lives revolved around their seven-pound bundle of joy.

No baby is going to rule our lives like that, we vowed.

Then we had a baby.

It didn't take long before our baby proved how naïve we were. His first night home from the hospital, he skillfully took control of our lives. For the first few hours, he slept peacefully. I was just beginning to feel as if I had entered "happily ever after," playing house with our new little family of three. About midnight, our cherub woke up and shattered my fairy tale. After eating, he started crying as if something life threatening were happening, and we thought surely he was trying to tell us something.

We soon realized we had learned everything about labor and delivery, but we knew absolutely nothing about taking care of a crying newborn in the middle of the night.

So between the hours of 12 and 5 A.M., Lynn and I took an on-the-job crash course in parenting. We spread all our books out on the bed and read fast and furious. We passed Derek back and forth, alternately feeding, changing, burping, rocking, and again changing this helpless infant. We could not understand why he was still crying when obviously we were meeting all his needs. The more we passed him back and forth, the more he cried. He let us know he was not pleased to be the guinea pig of our inexperience.

We emerged from that night bleary eyed but baptized by fire into the world of parenting. Only time and experience taught us that this fragile infant wouldn't break, that he could finish a nap with wet diapers, that when his immature nervous system was overstimulated, he might cry for no apparent reason. For the first few months, we tried to convince him that for everything there is a time: a time to wake up, a time to sleep, a time to eat, and a time to be quietly contented.

And I hate to admit that in no time at all, we became just like all the goofy new parents we vowed we'd never be like. We talked of almost nothing but our baby. We immersed ourselves in child-rearing information. We compared notes with friends, attended seminars, read how-to books, watched TV talk shows, and talked to more friends. We overdosed on the subject, and I still have two lasting dislikes from that period.

The first is the let's-compare-our-babies conversations, which are variations on the we-have-the-best-baby-in-the-world attitude. Despite our vow, we were pulled into these conversations, which seemed to occur whenever two or more parents gathered together. Inevitably the talk turned to whose baby slept through the night first, got the first tooth, or said the first "Da-da." Somehow these accomplishments always seemed to indicate superior brain power, though I'm not sure why. Similar conversations followed us all the way through preschool, centering on who knew their A-B-Cs or started reading first.

To me, these conversations seemed like brag-a-thons. They brought out the worst in me and gave me the first taste of what it feels like to wrap my ego around my child's accomplishments or lack of accomplishments, even though I was quite sure I had nothing to do with the late appearance of the first tooth. I usually ended up not liking most of these mothers (whose children were surely destined for the "talented and gifted" programs) or feeling terribly guilty because my children seemed so average and normal.

That leads me to my second dislike.

I dislike the hopeless, helpless feeling that it's too late to change the lasting impact of my mistakes on my children. Some things in life will never be theirs because I did not eat enough wheat germ when I was pregnant or read enough to them when they were toddlers or model enough patience when they were preschoolers. I used to fear they'd end up in therapy as adolescents and never get into the college of their choice. They are grown now, but sometimes I still fear they'll discover permanent scars in their psyches that will be all my fault.

In reality, I've come to the comforting conclusion that it's never too late to make a positive difference in our children's lives. As long as the Lord gives me one more breath, one more conversation, one more phone call, one more e-mail message, one more prayer, it's not too late. In that spirit, let's explore some ideas about loving and letting go of our children at different ages.

Zero to Two Years Old

Major changes in the birthing experience have taken place over the last three generations that definitely affect the immediate bonding between parent and child. When I was born, neither of my parents was immediately aware of my arrival. My father was down the hall asleep in a waiting room, and my mother was under anesthesia. I don't think that's had any lifelong effects on my emotional well-being, but it probably slowed their bonding to me, especially my father's, since he assumed that taking care of babies was mostly my mother's responsibility.

I know from my experience that bonding between mother and child begins immediately after birth. When our first child was born, I had to talk the doctor into allowing Lynn into the delivery room at the last minute. Having fathers in the delivery room was a new idea at that hospital, and I think he consented only because he feared I would get hysterical if he refused. He was right!

Together, we experienced the incredible miracle of our first child's birth. But after Derek was born, we got only one good look at him before he was whisked away to the nursery. Lynn was shooed out of the room shortly after that, and I was left alone, exhausted but wide awake, to sort out my thoughts and wonder about that mini-stranger in the nursery down the hall who would forever be part of our lives. The umbilical cord had been cut, and now, after being intricately bound together for nine months, we were separate and alone. I felt confused and ambivalent about our new relationship.

I didn't hold Derek until the next morning, and for three days he was brought to me only for short periods to nurse. By the time we got home, I didn't feel very confident or comfortable with him. No wonder we had such a difficult adjustment our first night at home. Our next two babies slept in bassinets next to my bed in the hospital, and I could cuddle or feed them whenever I wanted. We were already bonded when we carried them home.

Fathers play a major role in labor and delivery these days. From the moment couples announce, *"We're* pregnant," they participate together. Together they endure the nine months, God's perfect amount of time to prepare both baby and the parents for the birth. Together they attend doctors' appointments, listen to the heartbeat, and watch the ultrasound. Together they take childbirth classes. From start to finish, a father participates in this intensely intimate experience that bonds not only father to child but also husband to wife as he understands and appreciates the woman's role in this miracle. The father who watches the birth of his son or daughter reports that he immediately feels intimately bonded to his baby.

MOTHER-CHILD BONDING IS IMPORTANT

An infant's first developmental need is for attachment and bonding, fulfilled by the mother-child relationship. In fact, this bond is a baby's unique and vital source of security and trust in life. Studies have shown that a baby responds uniquely to a mother:

- Newborn babies prefer a higher-pitched voice. . . .
- Within the first week, infants recognize and are comforted by their mother's voices. . . .
- By the time a baby is five days old, he recognizes and prefers the smell of his own mother's milk. . . .
- By the time a baby is three to four weeks old, an observer can watch a baby's face and see the baby's unique response to the mother.[1]

In other words, babies need their mothers.

Other studies show that an infant's very survival depends on this relationship. In some extreme cases, otherwise healthy infants have died without the soothing love of a mother figure to sustain them. According to Dr. Henry Cloud and Dr. John Townsend in their book *Raising Great Kids,*

Research supports the biblical idea that relationship is crucial to life. Interactions between mother and child deeply affect an infant's developing neurological structures. The literal hard-wiring of an infant's brain, including such basic functions as thinking, relating to the world, perceiving, and judging, depends on the mother-child relationship. Severe disruption of this attachment in the early months after birth can affect a child's entire life.[2]

The fact is, the first year of life is critical to the development of attachment capacities in a child. Attachment must be solidly in place before any letting go can happen, just as nursing precedes weaning (in the more general sense of the word that nursing means nurturing). Bonding meets a foundational need in a child's life.

And don't worry that paying lots of attention to your child in the bonding process might spoil him or her. According to Cloud and Townsend, you can't spoil an infant.

People who say that infants are trying to manipulate you and need to be taught not to be selfish do not understand the absence of thought processes in babies. Babies do not even have the brain capacity to think that way. They are just in despair and need to be comforted. These stages are the foundation of their learning that grace can overcome painful reality. Love them out of their distress.[3]

WHAT TO DO ABOUT CONFLICTING ADVICE

The advice I've quoted from Cloud and Townsend is based on research about the developmental needs of children. But quoting these experts raises an important question. New parents are often overloaded with contradictory advice about all sorts of choices: whether to use a pacifier, when and how to start setting limits, whether you can spoil a six-month-old. A mother-in-law claims one thing. A TV talk show offers another opinion. Books, experts, or your best friend say something else. What's a parent to do? How do new parents know what is right? When it comes to choosing your style of parenting, my advice is to use critical thinking skills: listen well; read more than one resource or opinion; check the credentials of the authors or experts for their background and experience; and then test theories. Do they conflict with your common sense? Do they conflict with your values? Are they biblical? Do they work? Dump the bad stuff and keep the good stuff. Choose what is right for your baby and your family. You are the one in charge.

> *Use critical thinking skills. Choose what is right for your baby and your family. You are the one in charge.*

BEGINNING OF LETTING GO

For the first several months, a baby is 100 percent dependent on the parents. We show our love through our protection and nurturing and bonding. But mothers and fathers report feeling the twinges of letting go, even in the first few months of their child's life, in the midst of bonding.

One mother felt it keenly when she went home but had to leave her baby in the hospital nursery for several more days because of a minor health problem. Another mother noticed the twinge when she saw her baby turn over for the first time or hold a bottle, small acts of independence accomplished without her. One father distinctly remembers the first time his child smiled at a stranger, displaying the same grin he thought was reserved only for familiar faces. A mother working outside her home felt a painful letting-go tug when her maternity leave expired and she had to take her baby to day care so she could go back to work.

One of the most emotional decisions for a nursing mother is when to wean the baby. Pediatricians tell us one thing; La Leche League tells us another; and our friend down the street gives us a third opinion. Again this will be a personal decision. I nursed each of our children about six months and planned an overnight or long weekend away from the baby to finish weaning. These plans gave me something to look forward to and minimized the emotional significance of breaking this intimate tie with the baby. Regardless of the plan, weaning our babies was always harder on me than it was on them. This is true of most letting-go transitions.

For the baby, birth is the first separation experience, and experts disagree about its significance. At about six months, the baby begins to realize he or she is separate from the mother and may feel secure only when the mother is in sight. During this season of separation anxiety, try to build a feeling of security so that the baby gradually feels secure at greater distances and for greater time periods away from the mother. The trust established at this point becomes the foundation for autonomy and independence later in life, especially in adolescence.

As this sense of security is established, another need arises: the need for autonomy or independence. According to Cloud and Townsend, this is called "separation and individuation. 'Separation' refers to the child's need to perceive him or herself as distinct from Mother, a 'not-me' experience. 'Individuation' describes the identity the child develops while separating from Mother. It's a 'me' experience."[4]

The baby's physical growth develops in tandem with his or her emotional needs. The strongest bonding happens when the baby is cuddly and immobile. As the baby learns to crawl and finally walk, he or she is maturing and learning to feel confident at greater distances from the mother. One therapist believes that if the baby begins to walk too early before bonding is strong and secure, the child may later have trouble maintaining a loving close relationship with the parents.

Should the mother work outside the home during this critically important bonding time? That is a question with no simple answers; again, this is a personal decision, and families have to decide what's best for them. Many mothers have no option but to work outside the home; their choices involve finding the best, most secure child-care options.

I was blessed to be able to work part time from home during those early years, which was important to me. Yet I remember the reasoning of a mother who chose to stay home and focus solely on her young children but later worked full time when they reached school age. "I looked at those early years as an investment. I wanted to spend time trying to give them a firm foundation with the best love, discipline, and structure I could at that time. I think I have more freedom now because of my investment then."

Two to Five Years Old

As children grow more autonomous and less physically dependent on their parents, they begin a quest for independence. Born of this time is the term *the terrible twos.* Children at this age move around quickly, are self-centered, have not developed good judgment, and are bent on exercising independence at all costs.

At this age, children continually test the limits, and patterns of behavior formed now will last. If the rule is that the child is not to go out the front door alone, that rule must be strictly enforced, with logical, predictable, consistent consequences for disobedience. The principle is that actions bring consequences. Because toddlers are self-centered and interpret the world around them in terms of what's good for them, they learn to repeat behavior that is affirmed and avoid behavior that brings unpleasant results.

While setting consistent limits and maintaining discipline, we also need to acknowledge and allow rather than thwart our children's quest for independence. We need to allow them freedom in the areas where the consequences are acceptable to us. For instance, choice of clothing is a favorite area for toddlers to express their independence. They may be fiercely determined to wear Superman capes over their clothes every day, or a fluffy

pink tutu on a family outing. Generally, clothing choices are rel-
atively safe to let go and compromise on, although that sometimes means enduring the stares or disapproval of other less
flexible and understanding people.

Starting about age three, choice of hairstyle also becomes an

> *We need to acknowledge and allow rather than thwart our chil- dren's quest for independence.*

area of interest to children. I liked our girls'
easy short haircuts, but I'll never forget the
day I picked up three-year-old Kendall after
preschool. She was buckled in the car seat,
her chubby legs sticking straight out in front
of her.

"Nobody likes me," she announced in a
grumpy monotone.

"Kendall, whatever makes you think
that?" I asked in surprise.

"It's because I have short hair," she reasoned, matter-of-factly.

She didn't get her hair cut again for two years.

LET THEM MAKE DECISIONS

We must allow our children to start practicing the art of making decisions at about age two so they sense our confidence in
their growing independence and gain their own confidence in
their ability to make decisions. We start with simple choices: "Do
you want a peanut butter and jelly sandwich or mac and cheese
for lunch?" "Do you want to wear this blue shirt or this green
shirt?" Note that the questions aren't whether they want to eat
lunch or whether they want to get dressed. Don't give them
unacceptable options. We undermine their confidence in their
ability to make decisions if we give them a choice and then tell
them they made the wrong decision.

GIVE THEM APPROPRIATE RESPONSIBILITIES

The letting-go process is marked by the orderly giving of age-
appropriate freedom and responsibilities. At this age children can

empty their wastebaskets, make their beds, and keep their rooms in order. In setting these responsibilities, we have to choose areas where we are willing to be satisfied with less-than-perfect results. One mother gave her three-year-old the responsibility of brushing her teeth with no supervision. Later the child ended up with some cavities, and the dentist was concerned she hadn't brushed correctly. The mother realized she had given her child an inappropriate responsibility for her age.

This is a good time to start teaching good work habits and the ability to accept delayed gratification, which involves the understanding that oftentimes we have to do things we don't want to do.

EXPECT AMBIVALENCE

At this age, children are bound to vacillate between fierce independence and clinging dependence. This pendulum of moods can confuse parents and test their patience. The child who insisted on putting on his own shoes when we were in a hurry to get out the door to a friend's house was the same child who sat on my lap and sucked his thumb when we got there rather than joining the other children in the playroom. At home his independence irritated me; less than an hour later his dependence embarrassed me.

While children make strides toward independence, they constantly need to reaffirm their love for and attachment to parents. Children may become clingy when they feel insecure about routines, confused about their parents' coming and going, or pressured by overprotection. Forcing a child to do something at clingy moments only adds to that child's feelings of insecurity. Bernice Weissbourd, in a column on two-year-olds for *Parents,* describes the confusion of feelings about independence at this age.

> The tug that your two-year-old feels between independence and dependence may very well match the tug you feel between losing your baby and wanting her to grow up. You may subtly communicate that her baby ways please you,

and that you find her willful manner of asserting herself irritating. Without intending to you may then create difficulties for her in this period in which she is motivated to make great strides toward independence.[5]

Going off to preschool is a milestone of independence. Our children's preschool teacher encouraged parents to be sensitive to separation anxieties that might occur during the first week. She asked that we be prepared to stay with our child the first couple of days, if the child desired, to ease him or her into the new situation with security.

I took Kendall to preschool on her first day, fully prepared to stay with her. Some children were clingy; others marched right into the room and seemed unaware of their parent's presence in the hallway. Three-year-old Kendall, our youngest, walked into the room with an air of confidence and announced that I could go home now because this was *her* school. I left, feeling that bittersweet twinge of letting go. After all, I had planned on her needing me, and I felt a bit of rejection.

TALK ABOUT GOD

In spite of our children's introduction to school experiences, we remain their most influential and consistent teachers, especially when it comes to their spiritual training. When I began teaching kindergarten Sunday school classes, I learned some valuable lessons about what children are capable of understanding at different ages.

Children's sense of God and their ability to grasp spiritual concepts change significantly as they grow up. For instance, during the preschool years they view God much as they do Santa Claus: unreal and magical. They cannot comprehend the meaning of death and resurrection, because death for them is pretend and temporary. "Bang! Bang! You're dead!" they shout, shooting at each other with wooden sticks. "Now let's get up and play something else."

During preschool years, they eagerly devour Bible stories, but some stories are more appropriate than others. God's creation of the earth, stories about the first family, and stories about Jesus helping people and talking to children give them an understanding of the power of God and of Jesus' love for children.

Children ages two to five have simple trusting faith, and truth is anything we tell them. They don't reason, but they can begin to appreciate the idea of trusting God's promises by comparing Scripture with the reality they know: night follows day, and spring follows winter, just as God promises. We strengthen their spiritual foundation by teaching them they are children of God and loved by God.

> *Children have simple trusting faith, and truth is anything we tell them.*
>
>

In her book *Successful Family Devotions,* Mary White claims that young children are capable of understanding the following basic lessons:

- A concept of God—who he is, his character, his attributes
- Love and respect for the Bible
- Prayer
- Kindness toward others
- Obedience to God and parents
- Knowledge of the common Bible characters

White advises parents to use lots of visual aids, physical closeness, repetition, and brevity when teaching their children. At times, a thirty-second prayer may have more impact than a five-minute Bible lesson on a squirmy three-year-old.[6]

The first six years of a child's life are rich with the precious milestones and Kodak moments that fill the pages of family photo albums. Because of the dependence of small children, we are tied to them in a special way that is not duplicated again during

their lives. As they march off to elementary school, they begin a
new chapter in their lives.

ENCOURAGEMENT FOR MOMS

This season of raising young children can be the most fantas-
tic and the most frustrating for mothers, especially as we realize
that mothering brings out the best—and sometimes the worst—
in us. We know how critically important these years are in the
growth and development of our children, yet it's also a time when
we can get discouraged because we don't always see the results of
our efforts. We desperately need perspective and encouragement!

That's why I work for MOPS International (Mothers of
Preschoolers), an organization dedicated to nurturing the mothers of young children. "Mothering Matters" is our motto, and
through our resources, radio programs, and relationships formed
in MOPS groups, we help moms know that what they're doing
makes a difference in our world. Whether a mom works inside
or outside the home, whether she lives in the inner city, suburbs,
or countryside, whether she's a teen or a forty-year-old, MOPS
encourages her to be the best mom she can be. (At the end of
this book, you'll find more information about MOPS.) Just the
other day, I received a phone call from a mom who said, "MOPS
saved my life by helping me know that my feelings are normal
and that what I'm doing is significant!"

Moms are significant, and the early years in a child's life are
foundational to that child's future.

FOR REFLECTION

1. Letting go demands a gradual change in the way we show
   love to our children. What does this sentence mean to you?
   Over the last year, how have you changed the way you
   show love to your child?

2. What are some age-appropriate responsibilities for your preschool child?

3. What increased responsibilities have you given your child this year?

4. What increased responsibilities do you plan to give your child next year?

5. What are some of the sacrifices of mothering in this season? How are you staying connected to friends or mentors for encouragement?

PONDERPOINT

TOP TEN WAYS TO LOVE YOUR CHILD

10. Give lots of snuggle buggle hugs.
9. Be your child's cheerleader.
8. Create a sense of belonging.
7. Draw some lines and limits.
6. Show the way.
5. Let your child be herself or himself.
4. Get giggly and goofy together.
3. Learn to let go.
2. Take care of yourself.
1. Be a hope-bringer.[7]

8

The Middle Years

> What's the difference between a mother and
> a Rotweiler? Eventually the Rotweiler lets go.
>
> ANONYMOUS

I distinctly remember a moment of joy I experienced as the mother of children aged twelve, ten, and six. The details have grown fuzzier than the memory of the feeling. We were on a family vacation, and each child was at a "good age." Out of diapers. Able to put off needs for food or bathroom, at least temporarily. Old enough to appreciate the vacation setting, and young enough to still want to be together as a family rather than eager to get rid of the parents.

Ahhhh, I thought. *Let's freeze this family right where we are, because this is the best!*

If we divide childhood into trimesters, this middle trimester might be the most enjoyable period for parents. Elementary-school-aged children are more self-sufficient but are still eager to learn and are happily and securely tied to the family unit. Like the middle trimester of pregnancy, this is a comfortable zone, tucked between two more tumultuous zones.

This is an age of rapid change and significant growth when children learn to adapt and cooperate to get along with their increasingly important outside world. They begin to spend nights away from home without Mom or Dad. They learn to read, which gives them a sense of control over their lives. It is a time when we encourage their steps toward independence.

During this time, children experience a period called "latency," in which self-discovery and learning magically unfold for them. They become less self-centered; their understanding of right and wrong is based not so much on rewards as on pleasing God or someone else. They are more aware of the world of others. They understand sharing or they say, "I'm sorry," not because they are told to share or be sorry but because they want to please someone else. They learn that it's not always easy or pleasurable to do what is right.

At this stage children also begin to think more independently and structure their values. Even though we are loosening the reins a bit more now, these six- to twelve-year-olds still need training and reinforcement as they test their emerging values. They may question some of our concepts and values as they realize that parents are not always right and recognize that people around them live by differing ethical standards.

Early elementary school children are adjusting to all-day-long school, new webs of relationships, new adults in authority who have different rules and expectations, and many new structures. If they have had the security of structure in the earlier years and learned the importance of obedience, most likely they will try to learn to follow the rules now. Because structure and limits are important to them, the rules must be clearly communicated and understood both at home and at school so they will feel secure.

The child at this stage will also experience some yo-yoing between independence and dependence. Kendall, who sailed through preschool, began to fear going home with friends after school in first grade. She agonized over whether to accept an invitation and then often cried at recess or called, whimpering, to come home as soon as she got to the friend's house. Her insecurity puzzled and sometimes irritated me, until I thought about what else was going on in her life. Her grandmother had just passed away; this being Kendall's first experience with death, she was feeling confused and insecure. At school she was feeling inadequate because she didn't read as well as her best friend. Patience and understanding helped her grow out of these insecurities within a few months, which was according to her timetable, not mine.

Even a ten-year-old sometimes slips into the dependency mode. Since preschool, Lindsay had called me Mom instead of Mommy. During one dramatic, frightening moment on our vacation when she was ten, however, I suddenly became Mommy again. Lindsay and I were snorkeling together off a craggy beach when unexpected huge waves came up, crashing us into the rocks. "Mommy! Mommy!" I heard her plaintive cries as she looked to me to rescue her. Between waves, I reached her and grabbed her arm, and we crawled among the rocks to shore. We were shaken but safe, and I became Mom again.

Giving children new responsibilities during these years not only increases their independence but also helps to grow their self-confidence as we acknowledge and reward their capabilities. We give them new privileges as they demonstrate their ability to handle their new responsibilities.

Children now can share more duties around the house. In addition to making their beds and cleaning their rooms, they can load or unload dishwashers, empty trash cans, fold laundry, and feed their pets. The possibilities are endless, but don't overdo it. David Elkind in his book *The Hurried Child* warns parents not to overload children with too many responsibilities or with responsibilities that are too big. He uses the example of an elementary-aged child coming home to an empty house after school where he is in charge of himself, a younger sibling, and dinner preparations. These responsibilities may be too much and cause the child undue stress.

We equip our children during these years by helping them learn to make decisions, set goals and priorities, and think for themselves. We teach them how to communicate clearly and speak up for themselves when necessary. The patterns and habits they establish now will likely stay with them through the more challenging, unstable years ahead.

> *We equip our children during these years by helping them learn to make decisions, set goals and priorities, and think for themselves*

LET THEM MAKE DECISIONS

About age six, our children began making decisions such as what shoes to buy and what activities to join. Obviously they had adult input, but some choices were theirs. Our responsibility was to help them recognize the alternatives and the consequences or conditions of each alternative. For example, our daughter had a choice between two pairs of tennis shoes. Color was the biggest difference. I pointed out that the white ones might get dirty sooner than the blue ones. Did she want to live with that? She chose the white ones, which got scuffed on the way home from the store. I had to bite my tongue and curb my desire to say "I told you so!" She knew so.

If price was the difference (which it often was), we gave our children a different option. Because we paid for necessities at our house and shoes are a necessity, we offered to contribute whatever an average pair of shoes costs. If they chose a more expensive pair, our children paid the difference. That was their choice. We didn't tell them how to spend their savings.

One of the ways our children got spending money was through our lunch money arrangement. Hot lunch at their school cost $1.10. We gave them $5.50 a week. We also provided sandwich makings, fruit, carrot and celery sticks, and chips. If they chose to make their own lunch each morning, the money was theirs. They were responsible for posting and checking the school lunch menu, deciding whether they wanted the school lunch, and either getting the money from their envelope or making their lunch. The choices and responsibilities were entirely theirs.

A word of caution about activities: in trying to identify a child's bent or expose a child to a variety of interests, it's easy to "overprogram" children in the middle years—Scouts, crafts, athletics, music and dance lessons, computer camps. It's easy to overwhelm children with too many activities. In our home, we limited our children's activities; with a little direction, they weeded out the choices.

Help Them Set Goals

Setting goals helps motivate children to make decisions, establish priorities, and learn to aim for something with determination. We had a friend who dropped out of college because she was not motivated. Unfortunately she didn't have any goals or direction at that moment. She sat around pathetically for weeks, waiting for life to happen rather than making something happen. "If you aim for nothing, you're bound to hit it," as the saying goes.

Here are a few general rules for helping children set goals.

Be Realistic

Help children set goals based on their interests, abilities, and personalities. Although it is important to teach them to deal with both success and failure, we don't want to aim them toward failure by continually allowing them to strive for unattainable or unrealistic goals. They need a sprinkling of successful experiences to build confidence. Yet we should encourage them to dream. "Without dreams, you have no goals. Without goals, you have no dreams," goes the saying.

LIMIT THE NUMBER OF GOALS SET

Children shouldn't set too many goals; the goals should be specific and have time frames; and we should help them celebrate reaching those goals. To get them thinking about goals, ask, "Where are you now; where do you want to be a week from now (or six months from now); and how are you going to get there?"

One of our children was disappointed with a grade in reading. He set a goal to improve it. Because the grade was based on the number of books read and reported, he knew he had to read more books during the next semester. He defined an attainable goal. Next he needed to define steps to reach that goal. Getting an A in the class meant reading approximately a thousand pages. He had twelve weeks left in the grading period, so he had to read about eighty-five pages a week or about twelve pages a day. Then he needed a plan. He decided he would read before bed, but we knew and he knew that he always fell asleep when he read in bed. So we suggested reading before dinner each night. He agreed. With that plan, he broke his long-range goal down into weekly and daily goals.

Another of our children set a goal to swim in the city swim meet. It was a borderline attainable goal because we lived in a community of more than 100,000 people and only the best six girls and boys swam in each event in each age group in the city meet. We knew competition would be tough, so we helped her decide her favorite and best stroke and encouraged her to work hardest on that one.

In spite of her efforts, she missed qualifying for the city meet by two-hundredths of a second. She missed her goal by a hair, but she improved her skills; she learned something about perseverance and determination; and she learned to handle the frustration of coming up short.

MODEL GOAL SETTING

As parents, we model goal-setting and follow-through as we stick to a diet, a regular exercise program, or daily Bible study. We need to share our goals, successes, and failures with our children, so they know we all live through struggles with a combination of victories and defeats. As Dr. Bob Barnes notes in his book *Ready for Responsibility*, "Children need to know that just because a failure takes place doesn't mean it's time to call it quits. No, it means it's time to evaluate, make corrections, and then try again."[1]

As a family we set common goals and shared ideas of how to reach those goals. We tried to cut our public service bill by turning off lights and turning down the heat. We tried to watch less television and read more by declaring a No TV Day each week or by limiting our watching to an hour a day.

When Lynn turned thirty-nine, the kids and I decided to give him his fortieth birthday present a year early. Because he likes to travel, we made up an itinerary for a special family vacation, going to places he'd always wanted to visit. We made a scrapbook of ways we would save money for the trip over the next year. Each child made a promise on a page: eleven-year-old Derek promised to save aluminum cans; nine-year-old Lindsay donated a portion of her weekly allowance; and five-year-old Kendall gave up chewing gum. We had a garage sale; we cut back on Christmas and birthday presents; and we put all our change in a coffee can decorated with pictures and labeled "Send Lynn on a Vacation." As a family, we set a goal, defined steps to reach it, and worked together to attain it. We all kept our promises, and the vacation that took a year to make was the best we've ever had.

LET THEM ASSUME THEIR OWN RESPONSIBILITIES

The message here is, "Don't assume their responsibilities," which is a temptation because when we love our children, we want to shield them from the pain of accepting some of their responsibilities. There's that familiar example about discovering the lunch sack or homework paper on the kitchen counter a half hour after a daughter dashes out the door to catch the bus. You've told her time and time again to make sure everything is in her backpack before she eats breakfast, to avoid the last-minute panic that hits when she sees the bus coming down the street. Now she is gone, but the lunch is here.

We discussed this scenario in chapter 2. If you allow her to experience the consequences of this action, it frees you from the responsibility of nagging her or reminding her of the mistake— except when you want to demonstrate God's grace by delivering the lunch to school.

Here's another example of sorting through a problem and determining who owns the responsibility.

When he was twelve, Derek wore a retainer. The orthodontist told him to wear it at all times except when eating or exercising. In spite of my nagging, he didn't follow these instructions. During his monthly visits, the doctor could tell how much progress Derek was making and consequently how much he'd been wearing the retainer. I used to attend these sessions with him, and the doctor's scolding made me uncomfortable. I would make up excuses for Derek and then at home nag him all the more to wear the retainer.

I suddenly realized this wasn't my problem. It was Derek's. He was old enough to shoulder the responsibility himself. I surprised him when I told him that I would no longer nag him and that I also would no longer accept the consequences. He would have to go to the appointments alone. I had been acting as a buffer between Derek and the doctor. I had intercepted the doctor's remarks. When I no longer accompanied him, Derek owned the problem and wore the retainer more often.

I once heard a child-rearing expert advise parents, when determining who should take ownership of a problem, to ask, "Is it life-threatening or morally threatening?" If the answer is yes, parents should intervene. If not, the problem belongs to the child.

Apply this principle to the problem of cleanliness in a child's room. I have a sense of orderliness that our son did not inherit. Our ideas of clean differ considerably. He was perfectly happy to live knee-deep in clutter that offended me; but I didn't have to live in it. By closing the door, I didn't even have to look at it. It certainly wasn't morally threatening and wasn't typically life threatening. Usually a dirty room is the child's problem. One part did remain my problem, however. That was the laundry. (Doing laundry was and is one of my least favorite duties.) When cleaning his room, he often stuffed all his clothes in the hamper, which meant more laundry for me. Therefore, I decided he could own that part of the problem too. At twelve, he could start doing his own laundry, which he did.

Some moms simply don't like the dirty room and step in and clean it for the child, seeing this as an act of love. Dr. Henry Cloud and Dr. John Townsend caution against this, reminding us that parenting is about preparing a child for the future, and we enable rather than empower with these gestures, making our children codependent rather than independent. In their book *Boundaries with Kids,* they describe Allison, a mother who always cleaned her preadolescent son's room, because she loved helping him.

> But in many ways her helping was not "helping" Cameron. He had developed a pattern in which he felt entitled to everyone else's help, and this feeling of entitlement affected his relationships at school and at church. Allison had always been glad to help Cameron through the messes he was creating. Another undone project was another opportunity to love him.[2]

If we let go of assuming our children's responsibilities, we must also let go of our uncompromising standards. If we give them responsibilities such as keeping their rooms clean, we must allow the outcomes: we let them make their beds in spite of the lumps; we let them load the dishwasher even though we could do it faster and better. The results will be less than perfect, so we need to lower our expectations. Nan Chase advises that kids can start doing laundry at age ten. But, she warns, be prepared for "a few shrunken sweaters and accidental batches of pink socks. Parents should sympathize when these disasters occur, and utter the phrase, 'Practice makes perfect.'"[3]

Our goal is to teach them to assume responsibilities as they grow up, because the fruits of irresponsibility can render a child incapable of coping with homework, demands of a job, or even commitment to marriage. Generally, the way to reach this goal is not to regularly do for them what they are capable of doing for themselves.

LET THEM FIGHT THEIR OWN BATTLES

Fighting their children's battles is another temptation for parents during this stage. We rush to their defense at school, in the neighborhood, and with friends, teachers, or coaches. We'd be better off using discernment to determine when they need us to be their advocates and when they should learn to fight their own battles. This is sometimes difficult for me.

> *We need to use discernment in determining when they need us to be their advocates and when they should fight their own battles.*

ENCOURAGING A CHILD

I've often said that being a parent can bring out the worst in me. I can take it when people hurt my feelings, but if they hurt my kids' feelings . . . that's a different story.

I remember one such episode. We were spending a summer weekend at a large mountain cabin with two other families, which included two girls about the same age as our ten-year-old daughter. From the moment we arrived, it was obvious the other two girls had established an exclusive friendship. It was two against one.

As the weekend progressed, I watched my daughter's hurt grow deeper. Occasionally she caught me alone and complained they were being mean to her. Finally, the second evening, she found me in our bedroom and fell in a heap on the bed beside me. "Mom, they're being so mean," she whimpered, putting her head on my shoulder and crying.

That did it. I felt a mother-bear snarl inside me, and two little voices argued in my head. One said, "Don't get involved. They will work it out." The stronger one countered, "They have no right to be so rude. They should learn."

I listened to the second voice. After consoling my daughter, I marched out of the bedroom on my way to battle. I found the girls alone in the dining room, giggling and telling secrets. That fanned the final spark, and I ignited.

"I know it's really fun when you two get together," I said as nicely as I could (though it came out icily). "But do you girls realize you have hurt someone else's feelings this weekend? Do you know how it feels to be left out?"

It was over quickly. They mumbled something, grabbed some potato chips, and left. But it wasn't over. Unfortunately my daughter had overheard the conversation from the bedroom, and she was horrified.

"Mom, how could you?" she wailed, when I returned to the bedroom. "You only made it worse. Now they'll think I'm a baby and you have to take care of me. I could have handled it, Mom!"

Feeling calmer and more rational, I apologized. "You know," I told her, "there are times moms get so upset that they do stupid things, like I just did, mostly because they love their kids. I'm so sorry. Can you possibly understand?"

She nodded, reminding me of myself at her age when I decided no longer to confide my hurts and fears to my mother, because they always bothered her more than they bothered me. Her overreactions cut off some of our communication.

I made a mistake that afternoon with my daughter. After all, it was a typical ten-year-old girl's problem. At that age, girls seem determined to form tight cliquish circles as if they are oblivious to the feelings they hurt. Being on the outside helps one learn how painful exclusion can be.

My responsibility was to my daughter, not to the other girls. I should have encouraged her but not gone to battle for her. My responsibility was not to change the world for my daughter but to help change my daughter so she would be able to cope in the world. She needed to learn to confront the circumstances herself or accept the temporarily unpleasant situation. I had no right to shield her from that lesson.

BEING AN ADVOCATE

On the other hand, there are times when our growing children need us to be their advocates. An advocate is someone who pleads the case of another, a person who stands in support. When is advocacy appropriate? Here is a list from *What Every Child Needs* by Elisa Morgan and Carol Kuykendall:

- When your child is physically hurt by another.
- When a teacher misunderstands your child's needs.
- When your child is struggling to learn and needs to be tested or evaluated.
- When your child has physical or emotional symptoms of need.
- When your child confides a concern and needs help.
- When your child has been wrongly accused.
- When your child needs help expressing himself.
- When your child doesn't have the skills necessary to be an advocate for herself.[4]

Advocacy is inappropriate when we step in with the blind belief that our child is absolutely right and can do no wrong. Appropriate advocacy requires an objective view.

ENCOURAGE THEIR SPIRITUAL GROWTH

This middle trimester is a period of tremendous spiritual growth for children as they think more conceptually and move away from the fantasy concept of God. They begin to understand doctrines about salvation, grace, God, and Satan and are more able to accept that God doesn't always answer their prayers exactly as they ask. They learn that sometimes God says no or wait, because God gives us what we need, not necessarily what we want. Children learn we don't always get instant gratification.

During this period, a child may begin to tithe. Our church believes that children at age eight may be able to make a commitment to pledge a certain amount of money each week to the church. But they emphasize that this decision is up to the parents and child.

We first gave our children allowances at age five, with the instruction that some money was to save, some was to spend, and some was for God. They were responsible for taking a portion to Sunday school each week . We didn't nag or scold. Sometimes it was forgotten; sometimes they gave extra. Nancy Lloyd, author of *Simple Money Solutions,* notes that "kids who learn the most about money typically have some restrictions on when and how they can use their allowance. A portion can be spent right away, another portion must be saved, and a third portion is to be used to help others via charities."[5]

This may be the time children choose to make a personal commitment to the Lord. A fifth grader in a recent children's worship service at our church told how she asked the Lord into her heart.

For a long time, I thought I was born a Christian because my parents were Christians. Then I learned that I had to ask Jesus into my heart myself. That didn't sound too hard. So one night before bed when I was six years old, I asked Jesus into my heart. Both my parents were with me, and we prayed together, and then I went to sleep. When I woke up, I didn't feel any different, and I didn't notice that anything in my life changed.

It wasn't until this year that I began to realize I could pray and talk to Jesus all by myself, every morning and all during the day. I could pray for thirty seconds or five minutes, anytime, anywhere. That's when I began to understand the meaning of a personal relationship with the Lord.

Obviously there is no one appropriate age for a child to make a personal commitment to receive Christ into his or her life. It may be preschool or first grade. Cloud and Townsend note that "only God knows the child's heart and readiness." In terms of cognitive development, they note that a child needs to understand:

- The existence and love of God
- The reality of our sinful state
- The penalty of sin
- God's provision through the death of Christ
- The requirement of accepting Christ personally[6]

Parents may tell their children how to make a commitment to the Lord, but we must assure them that this is a personal choice and not pressure them. We can lead, but we can't get them there.

How do we lead? By slowly weaving God's truth into our everyday experiences and sharing the foundational truths of the gospel message. Ideally, this knowledge is shared over a period of time in discussions and through Bible stories and Scripture and devotional reading.

Our twelve-year-old son, on the brink of adolescence and tugged by peer influence, sometimes questioned his commitment to his faith. "But I want to have fun," he wailed.

Don't Christians have fun? I wondered. *Where does he get a scolding, scowling, somber image of a Christian? How are we modeling our faith?* During these middle years, our children watch us carefully and hold us accountable.

> *At this age, our children watch us carefully and hold us accountable.*

Referring to having a daily family devotional time, Dr. Bob Barnes notes the importance of modeling excitement about studying God's Word: "Be prepared to get excited about having devotions even if you seem to be the only one who is excited. . . . Children are probably not going to cheer over the devotion times, but that doesn't mean that their lives aren't being positively affected. The impact will be lived out rather than shouted about."[7]

WRAP-UP

As they teeter on the brink of adolescence at the end of this period, we're conscious of our children's changing bodies and minds. As we watch them mature, we may feel that familiar bittersweet twinge of letting go that comes with their growing up. I see chubby hands with dimpled knuckles become stronger and more capable. I watch compact squatty bodies stretch out to lean lengths. I notice they are spending more time in their rooms and less time lingering over dinner. They like the mirror, telephone, clothes, and CDs better, and my pancakes less.

Life is tugging at their sleeves . . . and my heart.

FOR REFLECTION

1. What do you enjoy about the middle years with your child? What yo-yoing between dependence and independence do you see?

2. Name four or five situations in which you are allowing your child to make choices. In each situation, what consequences of good or bad choices does your child experience?

3. In what area of your child's life could you help him or her set some goals? How might you encourage those to be?

4. Describe a time when you assumed your child's responsibility. A time when you fought one of his or her battles. How might you do things differently next time?

5. How is your child growing spiritually?

PONDERPOINT

THE "GIFT-LOVE" OF MATERNAL INSTINCT

We feed children in order that they may soon be able to feed themselves; we teach them in order that they may soon not need our teaching. Thus a heavy task is laid upon this Gift-love [of maternal instinct]. It must work towards its own abdication.

C. S. LEWIS[8]

9

Adolescence

If we impose our identity on our teens, we are, in effect,
thwarting God's best for them. God wants only the
best for His children, just as we do. But we have only
some of the facts, while God has all of them.

DAVID MCKENNA

"God made babies so precious and adorable so we don't mind
getting up at 3:00 A.M. to feed them, and he made adolescents so
obnoxious so we don't mind when they leave home."

Hearing that ditty years ago when our oldest was a delightful
ten-year-old, I laughed with little understanding. Then as he
approached thirteen, I had a far different appreciation for the
truth in that humor.

I look back on my adolescence as an unstable time. Peer pressure was painfully powerful, but my peers were as confused as I
was. I was torn between loving and hating my parents. I spent a
lot of time worrying about who I was, where I was going, and
what I wanted to do when I got there.

Adolescence is a tough time. It's an in-between age, a transition between childhood and adulthood when kids don't have the privileges and excuses of being children nor the freedom of being adults.

It is a time of struggle for autonomy and independence, much like the struggle a two-year-old faces. "An adolescent is a two-year-old with hormones and wheels," describes child psychiatrist Foster Cline, who sees many similarities between these two age groups.

> *The task of adolescence is to separate and ask the question, "Who am I apart from my family?" and to gain confidence in the answer.*

The task of adolescence, no matter how strong or close the family, is to separate and pull away, to ask the question, "Who am I apart from my family?" and to gain confidence in the answer.

For parents, adolescence marks the home stretch of active parenting, when we gradually allow our children to test their wings. It is a time when we consciously change the way we show our love for them as we command less and trust more.

For both kids and parents, it can be an emotionally trying time. "Separation is a mutual experience for adolescent and parent—both have to deal with the ambivalences and rewards of letting go," writes Michael V. Bloom in *Adolescent-Parental Separation*.[1]

Some parents seem to weather the adolescent years better than others. "They were rich, rewarding, challenging years," said one enthusiastic parent. "I thoroughly enjoyed our children as teenagers!"

Another disagrees. "Adolescence was one long fight for independence. My teenagers were moody, selfish, rebellious, and impossible to live with. But why should I be surprised? Fighting for independence is the American way."

What accounts for the difference in these experiences? Probably it's a combination of the teenagers' level of struggle and the parents' response. Let's first consider the parents' response.

PARENTS' RESPONSE

Three factors seem to affect a parent's ability to respond and cope during adolescence: the parent's attitude, understanding, and expectations.

ATTITUDE

"This may shock you," writes Charles Swindoll, "but I believe the single most significant decision I make on a day-to-day basis is my choice of attitude." For several years I posted this quote on our refrigerator door because it helped me when I faced circumstances I couldn't change—like my children's adolescence. They were on a journey to maturity and independence. To get there, they had to go through this season with all its moods and choices and dramatic rebellions, which I couldn't change or control. But I could change and control my attitude.

We can approach our children's adolescence optimistically with a willingness to listen, compromise, and display dogged determination. We can view the entire period as a stormy season to be endured as we brace ourselves against the inevitable conflicts. Or our attitude can be, "Given the task at hand, let's make the most of this period." We have power in the attitude we choose.

UNDERSTANDING

Understanding is our willingness to walk in our children's shoes and recognize their feelings and needs. Do we remember what it felt like to have an unpredictably squeaky voice or an acne problem?

How do we feel now when we have a bad hair day or show up somewhere wearing casual clothes when everyone else is wearing formal? We feel self-conscious. How do we feel when we hear about a gathering of our friends that didn't include us? We feel left out. How do we feel when everyone else around us in the exercise class can do fifty situps, but we can't get past twelve? We feel like we're not good enough. How do we react when someone criticizes the way we look, act, or think? In spite of our defensiveness, deep down we feel insecure.

Adolescents feel all those same emotions, only more intensely because they aren't as mature and experienced in coping with their feelings. We need to be sensitive to their struggles and their ambivalence in needing to separate from us but still be affirmed by us. To better understand what they face and feel every day, we need to listen, not judge, and empathize, not criticize.

EXPECTATIONS

Our expectations—both realistic and unrealistic—are based on memories of our own experiences and our hopes for the future, for the way we think life ought to turn out. The more we know or remember about adolescence, the more realistic our expectations will be about what life will be like during these years.

Adolescence is the time of transformation from dependence on parents to independence. Adolescents' need to separate from parents is real. We can accept and facilitate this need, easing the process, or we can thwart their efforts, making the process more traumatic.

Rebellion is often a normal part of this separation process, as adolescents define what they think apart from what we think. They continue to test, formulate, and build values of their own, and the process often hammers away at our values. They may reject what we think, but we shouldn't interpret that as a personal rejection. They are not rejecting us. In his book *Too Big to Spank,* Jay Kesler writes about adolescents, "To be young is to question and test. It doesn't mean they are hostile. It doesn't mean that they are going to leave the time-tested things permanently."[2]

> *Rebellion is often a normal part of an adolescent's separation process.*
> ❧

If we don't allow our adolescents to develop their individuality, they have one of two choices: to rebel dramatically or comply quietly. Neither is desirable. The dramatic rebellion may mean getting involved with the wrong crowd or even running away from home. Complying quietly may mean facing problems later in life.

A thirty-five-year-old woman described how her mother used to march her off to the hairdresser every six months until she was twenty-one years old for the same short bob and frizzy permanent. She detested the style and ritual, but it never occurred to her to resist her mother's control over her life. After graduating from college and moving away from home, she still struggled with the lack of self-confidence that had paralyzed her in adolescence.

"I didn't go through those normal adolescent rebellions until after I was married, and then it was painfully difficult to separate from my parents, to think of myself as an individual and gain self-confidence." She paused. "I hope my daughter experiences some rebellion in her teenage years because I know such feelings are necessary and healthy."

The mother of this woman expected that adolescence meant a continuation of the smooth sailing, control, and obedience of the childhood years. No changes. "In all fairness to my mother, she loved me and had no idea what she was doing to me by controlling me in that way," the daughter said.

TASKS OF TEENAGERS

As we've identified, a teenager's task is to pull away and separate from the family and gain independence. According to Dr. Henry Cloud and Dr. John Townsend in *Raising Great Kids*, teens are looking to:

- Think for themselves and have their own opinions
- Question, evaluate, and choose values
- Follow their own desires and goals
- Build skills and abilities
- Look ahead
- Develop their own spirituality
- Find their own ways of making money
- Have parents available to them while they are working all of this out[3]

According to researchers, adolescents strive for three forms of autonomy in seeking independence: behavioral, emotional, and values autonomy.

Behavioral autonomy results in conflicts about dating, recreational activities, choice of friends, curfews, money, clothing, and hairstyles.

Emotional autonomy involves self-reliance, self-control, and the transfer of emotional attachment from family members to peers. Close friends are extremely important to adolescents. They spend more time on the telephone and less time at home. They may form friendships with other adults—a coach, teacher, or neighbor—to fill the spaces of separateness they are creating in their relationship with their parents. Parents should see this as a positive step, not a personal rejection or a reason to feel jealous.

Values autonomy is the adolescent's struggle to define and claim moral and religious values, vocational choices, and life goals. It is a search for self-identity and clarification. Seeking values autonomy often results in the rebellion we've discussed and the questioning and rejecting of parental rules and values that causes emotional confrontations.[4]

As adolescents seek their autonomy and pull away from us both physically and emotionally, we need to understand that their

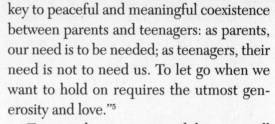

needs differ from ours. As Haim Ginott says, "Letting go is the key to peaceful and meaningful coexistence between parents and teenagers: as parents, our need is to be needed; as teenagers, their need is not to need us. To let go when we want to hold on requires the utmost generosity and love."[5]

> "*Letting go is the key to peaceful and meaningful coexistence between parents and teenagers.*"

Even as they tug away, adolescents still need the stability and reassuring warmth of our love. One high school counselor urges parents to fill their teenagers' emotional tanks whenever they are low or on empty and zoom in for a pit stop. They still need hugs, back rubs, and eye-to-eye conversations, even if the opportunities for sharing are fewer.

TASKS OF PARENTING

As we journey through the up and down years of parenting our teens, it's helpful to remember the bigger picture goals and guidelines of letting go.

LETTING-GO PROCESS

Using a mathematical analogy, a baby is totally dependent on his or her parents. On a scale of zero to one hundred, the infant has zero independence. Throughout the letting-go process, the percentage of independence gradually increases as we give them freedom and transfer responsibility from our shoulders to theirs. Our goal is to empower our children to be 100 percent independent at maturity, which means that during high school, they should be at about 75 percent. It's good to take stock. Here are some questions to ask yourself about your teenagers:

- Are they becoming problem solvers, thinking for themselves?
- Are they showing signs of good character—honesty, integrity, and the ability to deal with life?

- Are they making good choices and standing up for the right things?
- Are they able to accept responsibility?
- Do they take ownership of their mistakes?
- Do they treat others well?
- Do they have faith?

EMPOWER VERSUS CONTROL

We want to give our children a firm foundation of Christian values, a healthy ability to accept and give love, and a sense of initiative and follow-through. We want to empower them, not control them. Control means to have power over them by using force, threats, or manipulation to make them behave in a certain way. Empowering means to give them power and control over themselves. Here are some questions to ask yourself about your parenting. Are you:

- Loosening, not tightening, the reins as they grow?
- Giving more information and fewer commands?
- Teaching them how to think, not what to think?
- Allowing them to have and express opinions different from your own?
- Allowing them to ask honest questions and express their doubts as they seek to own their faith?
- Allowing them to experience the consequences of their choices?
- Avoiding control issues?

This last one bears more explanation because control issues are so painfully powerful and common during the teen years.

CONTROL ISSUES

Control issues get out of hand quickly because they center on the question, "Who's in charge here?" which usually means one person has to win (or be right) and one person has to lose (or be wrong). A teenager seeking independence does not want to lose. Neither does a parent seeking control. So the battle lines can be drawn quickly—unless the parent steps back and assesses the situation, remembering that total control is not the goal here. The aim is to empower the teenager and give some control, which is what the teen is fighting for. Here are some guidelines to help you sort through control issues:

- Maintaining the relationship is more important than being right or being powerful.

- A control issue is really a battle over "who's in control here?" and we don't need to win that battle. We can give away some control and keep some control.

- We can't force the teenager to do something; instead we tell him (or her) what we will do. That's where we have the power and control—with ourselves.

- We give him choices. He makes the choice (which gives him control) and accepts the consequences of his choices (which is how the real world works).[6]

WHOSE BATTLES?

An ongoing temptation, especially for certain parents, is to fight their teenagers' battles. Giving in to this temptation teaches teenagers to expect that Mom or Dad will always be there to make life fair.

I have a friend who is a high school counselor. She tells me about the parents who always fight their kids' battles, whether their kids are right or wrong. For instance, a girl is dropped from the cheerleading squad because her grades have slipped below the designated grade point average, or a boy is ineligible to suit up for the game Friday night because a certain teacher won't give him a higher grade on a test. These parents come storming to the teacher or counselor, demanding that an exception be made for their daughter or son because this is an injustice—just like all the other injustices they've protected their children from throughout childhood.

Granted, there are times parents must come to the defense of their children. Some injustices can't and shouldn't be overlooked, and we're challenged to make those difficult distinctions. The father of a high school student described the struggle he had with such a decision. "My daughter dropped from a straight A to a B in a favorite class simply because we were on vacation and she missed a day of school. According to the teacher, missing class for any reason other than illness was an automatic grading penalty. I wrestled with the decision of whether I should talk to the teacher. It was an unfair inflexible rule, but more important, I decided my daughter should learn that life is full of unfair rules I can't change. I encouraged her to talk to the teacher, but I stayed out of it."

> We rejoice in our sufferings, knowing that suffering produces endurance, and endurance produces character, and character produces hope, and hope does not disappoint us, because God's love has been poured into our hearts through the Holy Spirit which has been given to us.
>
> *Romans 5:3–5* RSV

EARLY ADOLESCENCE

Some differences in teens are age specific. Middle school students begin to show signs of maturing and separating. They may grow moody and seek more privacy in their bedrooms, which they decorate to reflect their personalities. Or they retreat to friends' houses. They bounce back and forth between dependence and independence like playful puppies, wanting attention one minute and growling the next.

The middle school years bring so many major changes in the life of a teenager that experts identify this time as a child's most difficult period. "Middle school years are probably the most stressful time in a child's life," claims Dell Elliott, behavioral researcher and father of six who has made a nationwide survey of adolescents. "Between the ages of eleven and fifteen, kids experience tremendous changes. Their bodies change, peers begin to compete effectively with parents for influence, and their concepts of right and wrong are being challenged."

When a child goes from an elementary school to a middle school, the structure of the system brings major changes. Usually they go to a different building with different schedules that require decisions about courses and extracurricular activities. Because of their increased autonomy, middle school students have more freedom to make choices and face more pressures and temptations than previously. Sex, alcohol, and drugs are issues they will confront. A national expert on teenage drug use warns, "The biggest mistake parents make is believing their children will never use drugs."

The consequences of their actions become more costly as they grow up, but this doesn't mean we tighten instead of loosen the reins. If they make mistakes, we turn those errors into opportunities for learning.

Because of peer pressure, parents may notice marked behavior changes in their middle school students. For instance, a girl who has been a model child may suddenly begin dressing differently—sloppy or punky instead of clean cut. Through her appearance, she is trying to make a statement to her friends more than to her family. The new look is not necessarily a rejection of parental values but an attempt to create a unique image as the teen explores the answer to the "who am I?" question.

According to Elliott, who also teaches parenting seminars,

Parents need to decide in which areas they will compromise and in which areas they will stand firm. For instance, we decided that on matters of style and taste, we will compromise. That includes dress, hair, music, and cleanliness of their rooms. On matters of values, we will not yield. That includes telling the truth and showing respect for others, which means they tell us where they are going and when they will return. As they reached adolescence, we gave our children more autonomy in matters of style, but we didn't budge on values.[7]

High School Years

If adolescents are two-year-olds with hormones and wheels, they come of age in senior high school. For teenagers, cars are the wheels to freedom. For parents, they are the cause of coronaries.

Having teens behind the wheel brings a whole new world of worries and responsibilities. They now make decisions that have greater consequences. Not only do they decide when to pull out into traffic or how fast to go, but the car also gives them the freedom to decide where to go and when to come home. Many parents put restrictions on car use. For instance, their teenagers must keep up a certain grade point average, contribute to the cost of the insurance, upkeep, and gasoline, and inform parents where they are going and when they will be back. "I don't want to worry, and I do want to know who will be home at 6:00 P.M. for dinner," one mother explains simply.

In other words, using the car is like entering a contract. Breaking a rule means breaking that contract and results in the loss of the privilege: no car for a specific period of time. And no arguing or nagging; we don't discipline them as we did when they were nine years old. We recognize their ability to reason, and we follow through with the consequences as they were defined. We are consistent and fair.

Our Role in Their Decisions

What is our role in their decision-making process? More and more, our role becomes advisory. Our goal is to teach them how to think, not what to think, so we contribute our thoughts as we help them explore options and consequences. Again, we give more information and fewer commands. Unless the consequences are life threatening or morally threatening, they own the decisions.

A family in our community has a son Eric, a talented football player, who as a high school senior was recruited by major colleges across the country as well as by the local University of Colorado. Choosing a college felt like a huge decision, not life threatening or morally threatening, but maybe life altering. His parents felt strongly about the outcome and offered their advice.

"We thought he should take the opportunity to go out of state because it was time to cut the cord and enter a new phase of life. But we assured him the decision was his," his father said.

Pressure increased as this high school senior traveled all over the country visiting schools. On the last night before he had to decide, the coach from the University of Michigan sat in Eric's living room, sipping soft drinks and talking about the opportunities for him in Michigan.

Eric decided to spend that night alone at his father's dental office, where he could think and pray about his decision. At the end of a sleepless night, he decided to attend the University of Colorado. His parents accepted and supported his decision.

The more we encourage our growing children to think for themselves, the more they care about what we think. They feel safe listening to our opinions if they know we won't force those opinions on them.

RELUCTANT DECISION MAKERS

Sometimes adolescents resist making decisions. A mother complained that her fifteen-year-old daughter had difficulty making decisions, even small ones such as whether to go to a movie with friends, what to wear to school, or what to order at a restaurant. "How can I help?" she asked.

When children need help gaining confidence in their ability to make decisions, we can assist by limiting their options. I feel overwhelmed with options when I walk into a wallpaper store. I need someone to narrow my choices by handing me two appropriate books of samples and saying, "Choose from these." We can play the same role with our adolescents by limiting their choices when they have trouble making decisions. For example, we can help them explore reasons why they might be hesitant to go to a movie with friends. We discuss their fears with them and focus them again on their options.

POOR DECISIONS

What if a teenager buckles under the pressures of high school? What if parents find their adolescent is involved with drugs or alcohol or engaged in unacceptable behavior and they feel they have no control?

I talked to a single mom who was in this situation. She faced every imaginable problem with her three teenagers. She felt at the end of her rope when she discovered a national support group called Toughlove, which operates on the premise that if we love our children, we must make them responsible for their actions.

> I was one of those mothers who thought it was too late. I'd done everything wrong when they were little. I was too permissive. I overlooked what they did because I felt sorry for their growing up without a father. This group made me realize that if I loved them, I had to teach them to be responsible for their actions and to expect to suffer consequences.

That was not easy. At age sixteen, her son began drinking. Time and time again, he came home drunk and passed out on the living room floor. Eventually he ran up debts, lost his driver's license, and even stole cars.

Through Toughlove, this mother realized she had to take care of herself and teach her son to take care of himself. She realized her bottom line was, "I will not allow a drunk in my house." That gave her son a choice. If he wanted to live at home, he had to stay sober. She would get him help and support him, but if he came home drunk, he had to leave.

> It tore my heart out, but it was the only solution to our problems, and it worked. He's twenty-one years old now, he's sober, and he's paying back all his debts. Not a day goes by that he doesn't tell me he loves me and thanks me for caring enough to be tough and help him become the person he is.

In this chapter, we've taken only a general look at the tasks and concerns of adolescence. It is important to acknowledge that some parents struggle with more dramatic rebellion during the teenage years. I know plenty of parents who are heartbroken and frustrated in their attempts to deal with teenagers who have serious substance abuse problems, are depressed, are irresponsible, or have disappeared because they claim they can no longer live at home. My heart goes out to these parents, and I encourage them to turn to sources offering more specific help and expertise, such as counselors and doctors—and friends for prayer support. In our small prayer support group, we've held these parents up with ongoing prayer and encouragement. Books, such as *Helping the Struggling Adolescent* by Les Parrott, can also be a great resource.

Spiritual Growth

What about the spiritual life of our teenagers? What should we be doing during adolescence to help our teenagers grow "in the grace and knowledge of the Lord and Savior Jesus Christ" (2 Peter 3:18)?

Ideally we would like our children to be active in church youth groups, sing in the choir, take leadership positions in church activities, and enthusiastically enjoy all of it. That's a mother's dream, but let's face it, that doesn't often happen. Many teenagers question, reject, or even rebel against the values of the Christian faith, and parents feel helpless.

The questioning in this area of their lives is no different from the questioning in other areas. It's part of the normal separation and maturing process. When they were children, they accumulated Scripture knowledge and parroted it back to us. Now they are trying to assimilate that knowledge and do something with what they have learned. And their questioning is not all bad, for two reasons. First, most experts agree that if a child has received a foundation of spiritual training, those core beliefs will guide the child through the storms of adolescence, and he or she will return to those values no matter what detours are taken. Second, we need to question our faith in order to own it. We internalize our faith through our questions. As we struggle with doubts and issues, we grow and reach a deeper level of commitment that unquestioning people never reach.

Distraught parents sometimes ask, "Why are churches losing adolescents?" If you ask the kids, they claim, "It's boring," or, "It's not relevant to our lives."

Should parents force their teenagers to attend church? Dr. James Dobson believes it is appropriate for parents to require teenagers to attend church with the family because "I have promised the Lord that we will honor him in this home, and that includes remembering the Sabbath to keep it holy."[8]

One father insisted his children be involved in something spiritual at least once a week, but he gave them options. For instance, if they were involved in Young Life, they would be permitted to miss Sunday school.

As adolescents approach high school graduation, they should be on their own, though living at home. I know one family who gives their high school seniors almost total responsibility for their lives. They do their laundry, budget their money, set their curfews, and make some of the family meals. "After all," the mother explains, "within a few months they will be doing all this on their own. And we want them to be ready."

That's our goal with our teenagers, and we do the best we can. After that, we lift them up to God, for ultimately we are not in control. I'm reminded of the prayer I said as I watched Kendall, our baby, get behind the wheel of our car on her sixteenth birthday, her new driver's license in hand. She waved, and then drove off all by herself.

> Father, entering that highway of real life right now is a treasure of my heart. I've done some things wrong; I've forgotten to tell her some things. But now she's out of my control, and I surrender her to you, asking for your loving protection, in trust and faith, even in the face of uncertain circumstances.[9]

FOR REFLECTION

1. Growing up, children go from being totally dependent to becoming totally independent. On a scale of 0 to 100 percent, where are your teenagers? Sixty percent independent? Seventy-five percent independent? How can you appropriately increase their independence?

2. Identify a control issue between you and your teenagers. As you step back and assess the situation, what is the real issue? How can you resolve it, allowing both you and your teens to have some control?

3. Do you allow your teenagers to have and express opinions different from your own? Why or why not?

4. On which issues do you stand firm with your teenagers? On which issues will you let them express their individuality or independence?

5. Is there an area where you need to exercise tough love? Explain.

PONDERPOINT

RELINQUISHMENT

To relinquish your children does not mean to abandon them ... but to give them back to God and in so doing, to take your hands off them. It means neither to neglect your responsibilities towards them nor to relinquish the authority you need to fulfill those responsibilities. It means to release those controls that arise from needless fears or selfish ambitions.

JOHN WHITE, *PARENTS IN PAIN*[10]

10

Facing Transitions: "Get a Life, Mom!"

> The parent must gain his freedom from the child so that
> the child can gain his freedom from the parent.
>
> MARGUERITE AND WILLARD BEECHER, *PARENTS ON THE RUN?*

"In this world, nothing is sure but death and taxes," wrote Benjamin Franklin a couple of hundred years ago. For parents, there is a third sure thing: Our children will grow up and leave home—eventually. It's part of God's plan for families.

Active, full-time parenting is a temporary job. Years ago I saw a circle graph of the average person's life span. The small wedge designating the child-rearing years seemed surprisingly skinny compared with the whole circle. Those of us immersed in this wedge often forget there is life beyond these parenting years. Yet just around the circle is the inevitable empty nest.

If you're married, here's another way to put these parenting years in perspective. Let's say you live long enough to celebrate your sixtieth wedding anniversary. Only about a third of those years are spent in active parenting and two-thirds are together with your spouse—without children at home. How we adapt to life without children has much to do with how we prepared for those years while our children were growing up.

As H. Norman Wright notes in *Seasons of a Marriage,*

> When all the children leave home and the nest is empty, some parents have no idea who they are or what to do with themselves. Their identity, both as individuals and as family members, has been so tied up in mothering and fathering that they are lost. They feel worthless and useful. They feel robbed of their roles and their children.[1]

We get all tangled up in our apron strings.

That's a warning to be heeded. Some of us weave our lives so intricately into the lives of our children that we have trouble moving forward. We get all tangled up in our apron strings. The process happens so subtly, yet so completely, that we don't even realize what's happened until we find ourselves teetering on the brink of the next season, unprepared for life without children.

Many years ago I vowed I would enter the empty nest era with a sense of purpose instead of confusion and despair. I vowed not to be one of those moms who kept following her teenagers around, doing things for them that they should be doing for themselves while they rolled their eyes at each other as if to say, "Get a life, Mom!"

While our children were in high school, I began to consider steps of preparation so I would not be surprised by the childless season of life.

LIFE'S SURPRISES

All of life is filled with changes that surprise us, even when we expect those changes.

SURPRISED BY MARRIAGE

I thought I knew what marriage would be like. Blissful. Romantic. Two people coming together as one. Before our wedding, Lynn and I went through the required premarital counseling. Our minister was patient with our nonchalant attitude about this requirement, which at the time seemed like just another item on our prewedding to-do list. After all, we had no big problems and anticipated none. We had starry-eyed notions of our happily-ever-after life together.

The minister must have read our thoughts as he opened our first session. "You seem well suited for each other," he began slowly, "but neither of you is perfect. You both have faults, and you are bound to irritate each other in the years to come. In fact," he continued, "as exciting as a wedding is, I wouldn't trade places with you for anything. My wife and I had some difficult times adjusting to marriage, and both of us agree our relationship today is much better than when we walked down the aisle fifteen years ago."

I listened with a bit of arrogance. *We,* I thought smugly, *will be different.*

We, I now concede, were no different. We found that opposites attract—until they get married—and a good marriage is just plain hard work as two people learn to live together.

SURPRISED BY MOTHERING

I faced the same rocky adjustment to mothering. If anything, this transition was more difficult. At least in marriage there were spaces of separateness. In motherhood there were none. Overnight I found myself constantly responsible for this infant who couldn't do anything for himself.

Nothing prepares women for that kind of dependency. Certainly not those experiments in high school where students are given an egg or a doll to care for as a preview of parenting. Here are the rules: you cannot let your egg or doll—your baby—out of your sight unless you arrange for a baby-sitter. It doesn't take long to start feeling put upon by the responsibilities of parenting. But at least an egg or a doll doesn't cry at 3 A.M. like a real baby.

Marriage didn't prepare me for that kind of dependency either. Lynn and I depended on each other, but let's face it, he didn't whine when I left the room or follow me into the bathroom and hang on my leg. Meeting a toddler's nonstop needs sometimes put me right on the edge.

Yet as I look back, I realize that, in some mixed-up way or by divine order, taking care of a dependent child also deepens our commitment, and over time, our love for our children grows as we weave the fibers of our lives together. Their dependency breeds bonding.

Though those years of dependency pass at a snail's pace when you're living through them, they zoom past, like a video on rewind, as you look back on them. We had three babies in five years, and now I remember myself looking like a character in a Charlie Chaplin movie, frantically racing nonstop through the days, trying to meet the needs of the one with the loudest demands.

SURPRISED BY "NO MORE CHILDREN"

Yet the day came when all the children were out of diapers. Kendall was close to three years old, and we faced a question all couples eventually must answer. Did we want to have any more children? I'd like to say this was a deeply prayerful process, but in fact the answer grew out of a gut feeling. Our family was full. We were finished. So Lynn and I decided: no more babies. The surprise was how I slipped into a terrible depression for a few weeks.

Even though I knew this was the right decision for us, I felt as if a precious purpose for my life was over. Parts of my body had fulfilled and completed their God-given function. I would never again feel life stirring within my womb. I would never again produce milk or nurse a cuddly baby. Since early adolescence, I had been aware that, as a woman, God was preparing my body to grow and nurture life someday. This decision marked the first step in being done with that purpose, and it felt like a major letting go. In fact, years later when I had a hysterectomy, I didn't go through any of the common emotional reactions. I had already grieved that loss.

> *We prepare them for life without us as we prepare ourselves for life without them.*

In time, I moved on. As our youngest reached elementary school, I felt thankful for the freedom her growing independence gave me. Going to the grocery store used to be the single major accomplishment of my day. Now I could squeeze a week's shopping into less than an hour on the way home from an evening meeting. Her independence gave me more hours to read, write, take Bible study classes, and invest in other relationships.

Time passes, and children grow out of their dependency as quickly as they grow out of their high chairs and swing sets. Year by year, as they inch their way to maturity, we gain more chunks of time to ourselves. The process of gaining independence is mutual. And it should be.

"The parent must gain his freedom from the child so that the child can gain his freedom from the parent," write Marguerite and Willard Beecher.[2] Letting go, then, involves two goals: weaning the child from the parents, and weaning the parents from the child. We prepare them for life without us as we prepare ourselves for life without them.

We've discussed the ways we wean children from parents. Let's consider some ways we wean ourselves from our children.

IDENTIFYING OUR SENSE OF SELF

Take our sense of self, for example. We must recognize that we are separate from our children. We have to separate our needs from their needs, our egos from their egos, and our emotions from their emotions. It sounds like a simple notion, but it is an area where we get subtly tangled in a web of interdependence. Sometimes while meeting our children's needs, we lose the sense of who we are as individuals.

MY NEEDS VERSUS THEIR NEEDS

Sometimes I have a hard time balancing my needs with my children's needs, assuming that if I respond to their needs and sacrifice my own, I'm being a good mom and a good selfless Christian. I sometimes carry that idea too far and get all mixed up about who I am and what God has called me to do. The reality is, moms have needs, and often our needs bump against our children's needs, so we have to choose to meet the most important need at that moment. For instance, to function well, I need exercise. But if I constantly give up my need for exercise (fearing that exercising would take too much time away from my children), I start feeling blobby, slobby, and extremely grumpy with little sense of self-worth. Not meeting my need for exercise is a disservice to the entire family.

Similarly, I need time alone with God and time alone with Lynn—every day. Meeting these needs makes me better able to do what I have to do every day. At MOPS we often illustrate this point by quoting the airplane safety instructions about oxygen masks: "Breathe deeply from your mask before assisting those traveling with you." In other words, when we take care of our own needs, we are better able to help those who depend on us. Also, when children see us taking care of ourselves, they're more likely to emulate that behavior and learn to take care of themselves.

VALUES

Knowing and maintaining our values is important, regardless of our children's needs or responses. Sometimes it's easy to give in and compromise those values to keep peace with our children.

I know a mother who compromised to keep peace around her house. She accepted rudeness and curfew violations and some dishonesty, just to avoid disagreements. She didn't stand up for what she believed to be right. She soon lost the definition of her values, and her sense of self became swallowed up by her children's demands. We have to stand up for and defend our values, sometimes confronting others, especially our children.

EMOTIONS

We have to separate our feelings from our children's feelings. We have to know the boundaries between them and us. Sometimes their happiness becomes our happiness. Their failures or rejections become ours. Their moods become ours. Many mothers admit that their feelings of personal happiness are linked to how well their children are doing.

I called a friend the other morning who was struggling with that issue. Her hello gave her away. She'd had a bad morning with her daughter Lisa, a beautiful, strong-willed child on the brink of adolescence. "She was in a terrible mood," my friend sighed, sounding drained and frustrated. "She pulled the silent treatment on me, eating breakfast without a word and leaving for school without saying goodbye. I feel just like I did when she was two years old and her mood could ruin my day."

> *My happiness cannot depend on my child's happiness.*
>
>

One mother admitted, "I'm only as happy as my least happy child." That may be reality for most of us, but we can reach for more stability. As the mother of a high school student vowed, "My happiness can't depend on his happiness."

EGOS

It's easy to get our egos tangled up with our children's egos. I know a woman who, though her daughter is only slightly overweight, fears that her daughter's appearance is a poor reflection on her. She constantly nags and bribes her to lose weight, making it appear that the weight problem is more important to her than to her daughter.

I know a father whose ego got tangled up with his son's progress in school. The teachers recommended that the boy repeat a grade to mature more for the next level. The father refused the advice and pushed his son ahead to the detriment of the child.

I recently saw a great ad on television. The setting is a state high school basketball tournament. One player, obviously the star, steals the ball several times, makes three-pointers, and seals his team's victory with a swish in the final seconds. The boy's ecstatic father is the first on the floor to share his son's moment of glory—and to introduce the boy to the sports agent who has witnessed his talent and now promises a lucrative future.

"But Dad," the boy says as he puts down the basketball. "I don't want to be a basketball player. I want to be a dancer." And he pirouettes around the gym.

The look on his father's face tells the story of tangled egos.

As we discussed in chapter 5, we need to check ourselves to ensure that our ego needs are not dependent on our children. If our children are our greatest achievement, we need to heed the red flag and seek new interests.

OWNERSHIP OF PROBLEMS

We must not let our children's problems become our problems or paralyze us with guilt. Too often, we play the blame game and allow ourselves to be declared guilty. He has a cold because I didn't remind him to take a coat. She doesn't get her homework done because she sees me procrastinate. They are bored and irritable because I won't take them to the movies. This is all my fault. Evelyn Christenson, referring to teenagers, writes, "Many times, as parents, we like to play God and give the impression that we are ultimately responsible. But as much as we might want to be, we're not."

Nurture and Protect Ourselves

Once we recognize the ways we get tangled up with our children—our needs, values, egos, emotions, and ownership of problems—we can identify ways to protect and nurture ourselves.

Boundaries

One of the first ways to protect and nurture ourselves is to set healthy and appropriate boundaries. According to Dr. Henry Cloud and Dr. John Townsend in their helpful book *Boundaries,* "Boundaries define us. They define what is me and what is not me. A boundary shows me where I end and someone else begins, leading me to a sense of ownership."

Boundaries, they claim, are essential to a healthy balanced lifestyle, and they recommend setting physical, mental, and emotional boundaries with our families and with our children.[3]

We first set boundaries with words. The word *no,* for instance, firmly lets another person know where we stand. We tell a child no to define the boundaries of right and wrong and to help them learn what is not acceptable to us. Saying no also defines what we are willing—or not willing—to do. "No," I tell my teenager. "I will not take you to the mall now because I have to finish this project. But I will take you in an hour."

We set boundaries with space. A closed bedroom door means, "Do not come in. Respect my privacy." Growing children set the same sort of legitimate boundaries as their need for space and privacy increases.

We set emotional boundaries when we clearly recognize which problems and responsibilities are ours and which are not. For years, at Christmastime I felt responsible for creating everyone's happiness. I was the self-proclaimed Chairman in Charge of Cheerfulness. As I learned more about boundaries, I realized I could choose to accept the responsibility of decorating the house and buying gifts and creating a nice Christmas (which I enjoy doing), but I was not responsible for everyone else's response.

Understanding boundaries helps us establish healthy relationships.

TIME ALONE

Spending time alone nurtures me. Time alone recharges my batteries, gives me perspective, and helps clarify my priorities and commitments. It gives me time to pray.

Some people seek more time alone than others. Some men regularly spend hours or days alone fishing. Other people hike or jog. I know a family counselor who deals daily with other people's personal problems and then faces the usual challenges at home as a husband and father. His secret for coping is to take an entire day or a weekend off alone several times a year, away from his everyday distractions, to sort through his priorities and redefine his goals.

When our children were younger, time alone always seemed limited. It used to consist of a precious few minutes early in the morning before everyone else got up, or it occurred coincidentally in the middle of something else: waiting a half hour in the car during a child's piano lesson; a rare morning at home where still, all too often, the phone, the buzzer on the dryer, or dust on the furniture interrupted and distracted me.

I used to be more intentional about seeking extended periods of solitude. One year I asked my family for the special birthday gift of a whole glorious day off in the mountains by myself from sunup to sundown: time to pray, think, read, listen to God, and once again redefine my answer to the question, "Who am I?"

In her book *Gift from the Sea*, Anne Morrow Lindbergh writes about spending time alone to gain perspective on her life and her relationships. The solitude was essential, and the seashore offered her analogies. "As the sea tossed up its gifts—shells rare and perfect—so the mind left to its ponderings brings up its own treasures of the deep."[4]

Rarely do we let our minds ponder for hours. Usually our thoughts are cluttered by the countless details that rule our lives and demand our attention. Yet when we are alone, we quickly get through that cluttered layer into the next level of more meaningful thoughts, where treasures exist. Time alone gives us an opportunity to redefine our sense of self and answer questions like these:

- What do I like to do? What don't I like to do?

- What brings me joy? What irritates me?

- What would I like to do with the rest of my life as a person, wife, and mother—physically, professionally, and spiritually?

- Where does God want to use me?

Now that our children are grown and gone, I naturally find more pockets of alone time. I take our dogs for long walks. I spend a Wednesday evening reading a book. I wake up in the middle of the night and consider the quiet darkness a sacred space of alone time because I can sleep an hour later in the morning.

NURTURE OTHER RELATIONSHIPS

We prepare ourselves for life without our children by nurturing ourselves and nurturing other relationships, including our relationships with God, family, and others.

RELATIONSHIP WITH GOD

The first relationship we faithfully nurture is our relationship with God. He should be first in our hearts, and we should experience his presence.

Different people have different ways of putting God first.

I need time with God each day. I try to get that time early in the morning. I sit at our kitchen counter where I can sip a cup of hot coffee and watch the sun rise while I read my Bible and talk to God. I absolutely needed the blessing of that time when our kids were little. I wanted the fruit of peace and joy and patience and kindness to get me through that frantic early morning rush hour when everyone was trying to get out the door on time.

Now that we live in an empty nest, I'm more flexible and spontaneous about my time with God. I've been known to carry on a God-conversation while zooming down the interstate, praise music blaring as I pray my way to Denver during my morning commute. Sunday morning worship, Bible studies, small groups, retreats, and prayer partners also nurture my relationship with God.

RELATIONSHIP WITH SPOUSE

The next relationship we nurture—if we are married—is the marriage relationship. In Christian premarital counseling, we learn that the marriage relationship takes priority over the parent-child relationship, but children can steal that place of priority so subtly that parents don't even notice they are strangers until the kids are gone. It's no wonder. By the time we diaper, burp, feed, soothe, and bathe our infants, and chauffeur, feed, encourage, counsel, and tutor our older children, we have precious little time or energy left to devote to our relationship.

The truth is, it takes time and effort to nurture a marriage. We have to care enough to carve out time for each other, even if that means sacrificing something else on the agenda.

Like all couples, Lynn and I could go days, sometimes longer, without an intimate conversation about something other than the kids and their needs. We started growing numb to each other. I sometimes didn't look at him carefully enough to notice the cut on his finger or his new shirt; I didn't listen to him, really *listen.* Suddenly we could sense it was time for dinner out alone together, or better yet, one of our overnight escapes. Overnight escapes can be either planned or spur-of-the-moment adventures. Over Christmas vacation one year, a snowstorm had kept me housebound with the kids for three days. I'd had my fill of wet mittens, drippy boots, and half-full cups of cold cocoa when a former baby-sitter, home from college, stopped by on Friday afternoon. She sensed the seriousness of my cabin fever and offered to stay with the kids. So on the spur of the moment, I met Lynn downtown after work, and we checked into a hotel near his office.

When we couldn't afford a dinner or weekend escape, we settled for a walk in the evening. Many couples regularly have lunch or breakfast out together one day a week, which is a scheduled priority on their calendars. The book *Ten Great Dates to Revitalize Your Marriage* by Dave and Claudia Arp has lots of ideas for spending short amounts of time together.

Longer vacations are more difficult to plan but worth the effort. One couple told us about taking a ten-day vacation at the place they had spent their honeymoon sixteen years earlier. They even splurged on a romantic day of solitude; they were boated to their own private little island. The boat delivered them to the beach early in the morning with a picnic basket and came back after sunset to pick them up.

"It's nice to rediscover why you married this person in the first place," this mother of two teenagers told me after their trip.

As romantic as all that sounds, I admit I had a hard time getting very far away from our children for very long when they were little, because I worried. Will they be okay? Will the baby-sitter use good judgment? What if Kendall gets sick . . . what if . . . what if . . . ? Even on a long weekend trip, it always took me about twenty-four hours to deprogram myself from my role as mother and focus instead on my role as wife. Yet we'd always return feeling rejuvenated and thankful to realize our children also benefited from the experience. They pulled together as siblings while we were gone and coped with responsibilities better than when we were home to assume those responsibilities. They also got a sense of security from knowing that we like to go away together.

As the saying goes, "The best thing we can do for our children is love our spouse."

RELATIONSHIPS WITH FRIENDS

Moms need friendships, and good friendships don't just happen. They take time and sometimes sacrifice, but they are worth the effort. Friends sustain us when we're down; they come to our aid when we're in need; and they enlarge our circles so we maintain a healthy perspective. Usually our good friends will continue to be around even after our children leave home. Friends are a good investment.

I know a single mother who sent her last child off to college and faced all the classic emotions of the empty nest syndrome. She was extremely lonely, but a solid group of friends pulled her through. They took her out to lunch. They took her on a trip. They helped her redefine her goals and encouraged her to get a job. One even dropped everything to spend a day riding up and down elevators in tall buildings with her to help her overcome one of her fears and gain new confidence. That's a true friend.

NURTURE OUTSIDE INTERESTS

As our children grow, we need to nurture interests and activities separate from parenting. As our lifestyle changes, we have to seek new outlets that challenge and develop the neglected parts of ourselves. Our children's growing independence gradually gives us more freedoms that nudge us in new directions. Preschool and all-day-long school mean freedom from getting baby-sitters; driver's licenses mean freedom from chauffeuring children. We can spread our wings as they spread theirs.

We can go back to work or change jobs; we can go back to school or volunteer or mentor younger women. We can start our own business, write books, take up golf, or organize a Bible study. We can follow our dreams. The options are endless.

For women who don't know what direction to seek, many counseling centers offer personality tests and interest inventories, simple quizzes that help determine areas of aptitude and interest. *What Color Is Your Parachute?* by Richard Bolles might help you discover your dreams. *Life Mapping* by John Trent describes a solution-oriented process that seeks to uncover a person's God-given strengths.

I have a friend who took a self-declared "sabbatical" after her last child trotted off to all-day-long school. She resisted the temptation to jump into lots of activities quickly and refused requests to chair committees or join boards. She took the whole year off to decide what she wanted to do and gave the venture credibility by assigning a significant title to this important period in her life.

I worked at home during our children's early years, mostly writing. As our children entered high school, I knew I wanted to find a job that would get me out of the house and connect me to other people. So I identified my passions—children and families—and sent off a letter to my friend Elisa Morgan at MOPS International. "If a job ever opens up there, I'd like to be considered," I wrote. A few months later, my phone rang. It was Elisa inviting me to interview for a new position at MOPS, and soon God's plan unfolded before me. That was seven years ago, and I've worked at MOPS ever since, encouraging the mothers of young children to be the best moms they can be. As I look back, I can see how God grew me along a path to perfectly fit this job he had saved for me.

One of my favorite Bible verses is, "See, I am sending an angel ahead of you to guard you along the way and to bring you to the place I have prepared" (Exod. 23:20). This is God's promise that he uses all the circumstances of our lives to grow us toward the place he has prepared for us. So in every season along the way, we can savor where we are, looking forward to what's ahead, because God will help us "get a life" in every season.

FOR REFLECTION

1. How did the role of mothering surprise you?

2. If you are married, how have children changed your marriage?

3. Do you remember when you realized you would not have any more children? How did you feel?

4. How are you preparing for life beyond your parenting years? How are you recognizing and meeting your own needs?

5. How are you tending to your relationships with God, spouse, and friends?

PONDERPOINT

SAMPLE YOUR DREAMS!

I'd like to . . .
Play the piano
Raise golden retrievers
Be an Olympic medalist
Open a boutique
Start a cake decoration business at home
Design children's clothes
Write a book
Become a professional photographer
Be a clown at children's birthday parties
Have my own .com on the Internet
List your own possibilities: _____ [5]

11

Fuzzy Release

> There is a time for everything, and a season for every activity under heaven: a time to be born and a time to die, a time to plant and a time to uproot.
>
> ECCLESIASTES 3:1–2

It is time to uproot.

This is the moment we've anticipated for years, sometimes with joy, sometimes with dread. It is the moment of final release. The eaglet is ready to fly. The apron strings are ready to be cut. It is a momentous, life-altering, Kodak moment.

There's only one problem. No one seems to know exactly when the moment occurs. There is no official ceremony, no retirement party for parents, no picture for the photo album that marks that moment when the final cord is cut. After all these years of preparation, the final release is fuzzy and undefined.

Maybe that's our fault as parents. Even though our job description slowly changes, we don't get a title change or a promotion or a plaque or a special pin.

"Once a parent, always a parent," one mother said.

"As a parent, you never cross the finish line," another said.

"No matter where your children are, they grip your heart forever."

I remember the day I was overdue with our first child and a grandmotherly woman gently took my arm in the checkout line at the grocery store. She must have recognized my impatience and fatigue.

"Your first?" she questioned, motioning to my balloon belly.

I nodded.

"Enjoy these last few days," she advised with a knowing smile. "You will never again be as free as you are right now. Once you have children, no matter how old they are or where they live, you will always be concerned about them."

Three children and many years later, I understand what she meant. We let go of our children, moment by moment, one by one, but we never really finish being parents. Our responsibilities change, but our love for them never changes.

Maybe the fuzzy release is our culture's fault. We have no rituals or rites of passage that clearly set children on their own at a certain moment. In past generations, parent-child separation proceeded with more continuity between adolescent and adult responsibilities. In an agrarian society, children assumed more responsibilities at a younger age. They may have married earlier, but they moved next door instead of halfway across the country. Often they continued to work within the family structure. The family still gathered for the traditional Sunday dinners and counted on one another for support.

In our times, release is so fuzzy that even parents and children don't agree when it occurs. When one group of eighteen-year-olds and their parents was asked if the adolescents were independent, the majority of youths answered yes; the majority of parents answered no.[1]

Or maybe the fuzzy release is the children's fault. We don't know when they are gone because they keep coming back. For years they're half in and half out, moving back home after months or years on their own.

One father assumed he was cutting the final cord when he left his eighteen-year-old daughter at her college dormitory on the West Coast, halfway across the country from their home. Four years later, he realized that was not the final cord. After her graduation, she returned home for a brief visit, packed up the contents of her bedroom, loaded her car, and pulled out of the driveway—alone—to go to a job in Washington, D.C.

"This time it's different," he reported a few days later, emotion quivering his voice. "This time she's really leaving."

A year later, he again wasn't so sure. "Emotionally she seems to need us more this year than she ever did in college. She is not surrounded by a group of supportive friends, and she calls home several times a week."

A few years later, he walked her down the aisle at her wedding and blinked back the tears. "This is it," he said later.

Well, you never know. By time she was thirty, she and her husband had returned to their hometown and settled in a house a few blocks from her parents.

COLLEGE YEARS

Separation in our society generally takes place between the ages of eighteen and the early twenties. For many adolescents, these are the college years, identified by one father of six grown children as the most difficult in the separation process, at least for parents. "If the child is in college," he explains, "your financial investment in that child is greater than ever before. Yet your control and knowledge of what the child is doing is less than ever before. We found that period extremely frustrating, but the kids didn't. They were blissfully ignorant of the stress they were causing us."

This father went on to explain that they did place one condition on their financial support. "We expected our children to get passing grades. If they didn't, we no longer paid their college tuition."

The college years include those memorable and confusing visits home when a child breezes back into the same house with the same parents and with the same siblings after living in an entirely different environment with a different set of standards and total freedom. The circumstances almost always breed disaster. It's the simple problem of differing expectations. The parents are hungry for descriptions of college life and eager to make up for lost time. They visualize leisurely evenings around the dinner table and even plan menus of favorite foods.

The student, on the other hand, who recently became a vegetarian and doesn't know how to break the news to his parents, visualizes mornings of sleeping late and evenings of time with his friends. Usually by the end of such a vacation, tempers have flared, feelings are wounded, tears are shed, and everyone feels ambivalent.

> *"My parents tried to parent me too much when I came home from college."*

"I expected a warm affectionate daughter who missed home, and what I got was a young lady who didn't want her parents to interfere with her life anymore," one mother said after her daughter's first visit home.

One daughter reported, "My parents tried to parent me too much when I went home. Suddenly after being totally on my own for three months, I had a curfew and obligations."

In our own household, I felt like the nutrition policeman had arrived when our daughter came home from college. Suddenly each can and box of food in our pantry was carefully scrutinized for additives and preservatives; many were deemed unacceptable, thanks to a college health class and a few new friends. Our son went through many the-hair-defines-me stages, from a shaggy look to a ponytail to a buzz cut. We never knew which one was going to walk in the front door during college vacations.

Who is this person? I wondered each time our children came home.

Like the rebellion of the high school student, these behaviors are part of a transitional phase, the search for the answer to the question, "Who am I now that I'm not a child anymore?" Much of the tension melts away through the college years as the student grows more confident and secure in his or her independence. The parents' challenge at this time is to let go of outdated expectations and minimize the confrontations on issues that are not morally threatening or life threatening.

As parents, we are learning to change the way we show our love.

WEDDING BELLS

The marriage of a son or daughter is supposed to mark the final step in the letting-go process, but parents and offspring seem to differ on the finality of that step and have differing emotional reactions to the occasion. One mother felt an emotional tug when her future daughter-in-law started taking over some of her former privileges and responsibilities, such as helping her son shop for new clothes or sewing a missing button on his shirt.

In our family, Derek was the first to get married, and we all kind of bumped around, trying to adjust to the changes in our relationships. Even Derek's sisters felt unsure of what his marriage would mean to our family structure. "Does this mean I can't call him anymore and leave dumb messages on his answering machine?" Kendall asked with tears in her eyes. He's now been married two years, and we are still finding our places in this new but good relationship. We've accepted the fact that he and his wife won't always be home for Christmas or Thanksgiving, and again, we are learning that in a growing family, love lets go of the old to make way for the new.

Derek's marriage reminds me of my own fuzzy separation from my family.

I felt only a small snip of the cords on my wedding day. I was pretty distracted with all the hectic preparations and prenuptial activities. After the wedding and reception, Lynn and I left immediately for our honeymoon, and a few days later I felt strangely sad at the distance between my family and me. They had worked so hard on our wedding plans, and I felt cut off from them and unable to thank them. Believe it or not, I had a twinge of homesickness on our honeymoon.

We spent the summer in Washington, D.C., and then returned to our hometown of Boulder, Colorado, where Lynn finished law school and I worked. Although we had our own apartment, it was almost as if we were playing house. Both our families lived in Boulder, and it didn't feel like much had changed in our relationships. If we joined them for dinner, we felt like children in their homes again. We felt certain obligations and responsibilities.

Our first married Christmas, my whole family—minus me— traveled to California to be with my sister and her family. For the first time, I didn't spend Christmas with them, and I felt painfully left out. Even though I loved my husband and his family, I wallowed in self-pity most of the day.

It was not until a couple of years later, however, that I felt the most dramatic cutting of a cord in the parent-child relationship. After Lynn graduated from law school, we boxed up all our worldly possessions, ready for a four-year stint in the navy that would take us to Rhode Island, Chicago, and San Diego. We drove out of town at dusk, headed east, and I watched the full moon rise over the horizon with tears in my eyes. "My parents and I will always watch the same moon in the same sky, but it will never be the same," I told myself. "From now on, we'll be separate in a new way."

And it never was the same. When we returned to make our home in the same town four years later, we had a child. That made a huge difference. Finally we were a family with legitimate obligations to each other that took priority over our obligations as children to our parents.

During our four-year absence, Lynn and I had grown up and grown together. Undoubtedly the physical separation from our families had helped. We felt safely and securely emancipated. We were ready for the comfortable status of an adult-to-adult relationship with our parents, partly because we now shared a common role as parents.

Usually the arrival of the first grandchild causes one of two changes in the parent-child relationship: (1) the new parents suddenly feel on equal footing with their parents because they now understand and appreciate the responsibilities and sacrifices of parenting, or (2) the new baby causes friction between the generations as the grandparents criticize the way their child is raising their grandchild. We experienced the first. Although our parents sometimes slipped back into the parental role, and although we sometimes slipped back into the guilty-child responses, generally we had cut the apron strings.

> *The period of fuzzy release grows fuzzier when adult children move back home.*
>
>

RETURNING TO THE NEST

The period of fuzzy release may grow even fuzzier when adult children move back home after being on their own. These are usually uncharted waters for both parents and adult children.

Many different needs bring young adults home to roost after they have been away. Sometimes called boomerang kids or bungee cord kids, these adult children move back home or stay home to live with parents, often to save money.

Regardless of the reason, the situation sets up many new challenges and requires adjustments within the family. Some of these depend on whether the young adult is moving home alone or with a spouse and children and on whether siblings are still living at home.

The situation works best with planning. First, the parents must consider their attitude about the living arrangement. They have a choice. Do they take the child back, or insist he or she makes it alone? Some parents resist the arrangement, fearing their children will become too dependent if they move back home. Others believe, like Robert Frost, that "Home is the place where, when you go there, / They have to take you in."[2]

In our case, Kendall, our youngest, moved home after graduating from college. We all knew it was a temporary situation while she looked for a job and planned her wedding; she would be married in less than a year. She worked at some temporary jobs, including a stint at MOPS. We made dinner together, took long walks with our dogs, and went to church as a family of three. I think we'll always savor the memory of that time as a precious gift—a context for our relationship that will never happen in the same way again.

If you are considering the possibility of a child moving back home, examine your motives. If a possessive parent looks forward to taking care of his or her child again or expects companionship through the arrangement, it's bound to cause conflicts.

Also discuss beforehand the conditions of the living arrangement. What are the rules and expectations? Will the child contribute to room and board? If the adult child has a job, many parents insist on at least partial payments. If the adult child has no source of income, parents may insist on a plan of action to assure that he or she finds a job. This may include going back to school, getting specialized training, or simply searching for work for a certain number of hours a day. The parents may ask the child to contribute to the workload around the house: do some laundry, help clean, and fix one or two meals a week.

Does the adult child living at home have complete freedom, or do the parents still have some authority? Maybe the child is responsible for his or her own decisions but agrees to abide by the family rules and values system, especially if younger siblings are still living at home.

If handled correctly, this time with adult children can be a time of emotional and spiritual growth within the family as parents and children learn to adjust and offer each other support in time of need. If handled incorrectly, the move home could make the adult child more dependent on the parents or could cause long lasting rifts in the relationship. At best, this arrangement should be viewed as temporary, just another step in the journey toward independence.

ADULT-TO-ADULT FRIENDSHIPS

After adolescents graduate from high school and leave home, our aim is to develop an adult-to-adult relationship with them. No longer should we try to scold, shape, or change them. Those parenting responsibilities are over, which gives us freedom to build a new friendship with them.

Consider the potential for such a friendship. After all, we have a shared history of memories made together. We were there when our children were becoming who they are. But the challenges are tucked in here too. That same knowledge means we know each other's vulnerabilities. We know how to push each other's buttons. And all too often, we don't accept changes and allow our children to be who they are today rather than who they used to be in high school. Or who we hoped they'd be as adults.

That many parents and children never achieve this healthy adult-to-adult friendship is evidenced by the parent-child relationships we see all around us. Watch the response when a young adult announces his or her mother is coming to town for a weeklong visit. The news is almost always met with sympathetic groans. A strained relationship with a mother is the brunt of many jokes on TV sitcoms and talk shows.

In a survey of 2,600 adults, 89 percent claimed to have long-term strained relationships with their parents. Nearly half of them complained their parents were still overprotective.[3] This indicates to me that we aren't releasing our grown children, even as our parents didn't release us; we aren't creating new adult-to-adult relationships with them.

STUMBING BLOCKS IN ADULT-TO-ADULT FRIENDSHIPS

What is standing in our way?

TREATING THEM LIKE CHILDREN

Maybe our little habits subtly tell them that we are still the parents and they are still the children. We still want to tell them how to live their lives. We still want to be in control. Often we communicate this without even realizing that our words make them feel like children. "Wear your coat. Buckle your seat belt. You need to eat more vegetables . . . get more sleep . . . return your phone calls . . . get back to church. You shouldn't get a dog now! You can't pay that much for rent!"

I've found that asking myself a few questions usually helps me recognize when I'm slipping into my I-am-your-mother-so-you-need-to-listen-to-me voice. First, how would I feel if my mother said that to me? Would I say that to a friend? Will these comments really cause them to change their behavior? Will they have a positive effect? If the answers are no, the action should be obvious. I should keep my mouth closed. But I have to admit, sometimes those words come out before I can catch them. Why? Because I am still a mother . . . who is trying to learn and change and let go . . . and not always succeeding.

"Parents who once confidently directed their children's lives, parents who once firmly voiced disapproval of their children's style of living, often come to a point where love and appreciation for respect and kindness win out over attitudes of judgment," writes Evelyn Bence in *Leaving Home*.[4] Do we allow them to be adults, or do we freeze them in their childhood roles?

BREEDING GUILT

Another major stumbling block to healthy adult relationships with our children is the subtle but powerful way we sometimes produce feelings of guilt in our adult children. We send them on guilt trips.

Breeding guilt is a form of bribery, an attempt to manipulate or control our adult children's behavior. The tactics may vary, but the results are always the same: the adult child feels guilty because he or she did not please the parents, just as in childhood when doing something wrong made the child fearful of losing the parents' love. The adult child recognizes this helpless childlike feeling but doesn't know how to deal with it.

Take this example, a phone call from an adult child to her mother.

"Hello," the daughter says when the mother answers.

"Well, hello," the mother responds, feigning surprise. "It's been a long time since I've heard from you . . . I thought you forgot my phone number."

"Oh . . . I've been busy," the daughter responds defensively, trying to make excuses.

Instead of being happy to hear from her daughter, the mother scolds her for not calling sooner. The adult daughter feels like the naughty child, and for the rest of the conversation, she's on the defensive. The mother's tactic doesn't make the daughter want to call more often, which is the mother's intent. Just the opposite happens. The daughter knows she hasn't pleased her mother. She feels angry and frustrated and vows not to call for a long time.

As an adult daughter, I lived through many similar experiences. I vowed that when my children grew up and called home, I would be honest rather than sarcastic. I would tell them I was happy to hear from them. If they had been out of touch for a longer than usual amount of time, I might admit, "I worry and wonder about you when we haven't talked for a while." That's the more honest message.

Of course now that my children are grown up, I must confess that I sometimes slip. But I have an accountability factor. They won't let me get away with guilt trips.

"G-T! Guilt Trip, Mom!" they tell me without hesitation whenever they feel I'm heading in that direction.

Another manipulative, guilt-producing gesture is giving a gift with strings attached. Usually it's a bribe for attention. Sometimes it's a ploy for power: "One can dominate others through gifts," writes Paul Tournier.[5] The gift of a plane ticket home every Christmas carries with it the obligation of time—and the sacrifice of the child's establishing his or her own family traditions. What if the child asks for the same plane trip home in March instead? Is the offer good only if it fulfills the parents' expectations of what Christmas should be?

The gift of money often comes with strings attached. "Our son and his wife needed money because they were broke, and the rent was due," one father recalls. "We gave them money, expecting they would use it for the rent. They didn't. Instead, they went out and bought something we didn't think they needed. We were upset for months. Finally we reached the conclusion that if we chose to give them money, we couldn't dictate how that money should be spent. It has to be a gift, given by choice. And we have to respect their choice of how to spend it."

Our goal is to give advice or gifts out of concern for our children's well being, not to continue our position of power over them. We admit that we make mistakes and that they make mistakes, like forgetting to call, and we aim to forgive each other openly and easily. We don't depend on them to satisfy our needs. We encourage and acknowledge their freedom.

PARENTAL GUILT

There's another side to the subject of guilt in the parent-child relationship. This is the guilt a parent feels when a child does not grow up the way the parent had hoped or expected.

Elinor Lenz notes: "Our assumption that parents are all-powerful and therefore all-responsible for what their children become has created a climate in which guilt and recrimination are as inevitable as death and taxes."[6] This disappointment can cause a paralyzing painful guilt that drains the joy out of parents and blocks their ability to move forward to all God has for them in the next season of life.

You name your child John or Luke and dream of how he will grow up like his biblical namesake. But instead, your son is rebellious and ungrateful and questions his faith and all your values. "Where did we go wrong?" you ask.

From the moment your daughter is born, you imagine the godly woman she will become. You take her to Sunday school; you gladly give up many of your own pursuits so you can be available during her growing-up years. But now she is seventeen and pregnant and unmarried and totally unconcerned about it. "Where did we go wrong?"

Here is the reality I've slowly come to understand: we are responsible to be involved in the *process* of raising our children, but we are not responsible for the *results*.

> We are responsible for their training when they are young and dependent on us.
>
> We are responsible for giving them limits.
>
> We are responsible for planting the seeds of faith in their hearts.
>
> We are responsible for helping them discover their uniqueness.
>
> We are responsible for loving them unconditionally.

The list could go on. But the last responsibility is the responsibility of trusting God with the results. We are not responsible for the outcome of our efforts. We don't control the temperament with which our children are born. We don't entirely control their circumstances as they grow up. We do not control the will of our children. They have free will, as we do. They will eventually make their own choices.

If we disagree with those choices or their behavior, we don't condone it, support it, or bail them out. We don't send money to support a son's drug habit. We don't allow a daughter to use the bedroom in our home to sleep with the boyfriend who shares her apartment in another city.

> *Our children are not our report cards.*

But we are also responsible to trust God and let go and recognize that our children are responsible for their choices and actions as they reach adulthood. Surely we make mistakes in child rearing. All parents do. We wish we had done some things differently; we wish we'd had the biblical knowledge then that we do now. But the Lord forgives us and promises to restore those years we fear we wasted. "I will restore to you the years which the swarming locust has eaten" (Joel 2:25 RSV).

Our children are not our report cards, and recognizing this truth helps us to let go and to acknowledge and celebrate their freedom and our freedom during the ups and downs and ins and outs of their fuzzy release.

FOR REFLECTION

1. Look back on your experience of leaving home. Describe some scenes or moments of release from your parents. Did you experience a moment of final release? Explain.

2. Have you experienced feelings of guilt as an adult child in your relationship with your parents? Explain. As a result of those examples, how will you treat your adult children differently than the way your parents treat you?

3. How could you improve your relationship with your parents?

4. Repeat this sentence. "I am not responsible for the way my children turn out." Do you agree or disagree? Why?

5. Describe the adult-to-adult relationship you have (or hope to have) with your children. Can you improve it? How? Or what can you do now to assure that kind of relationship in the future?

PONDERPOINTS

No Promises

I'm going to make a statement that may disturb some who prefer strict, predictable, hard-and-fast formulas for living. *There is no guarantee when it comes to rearing a child.* ... As much as we would love to have airtight assurance that if we only use this or that parenting method, everything will turn out right—we simply cannot have that assurance. I can't tell you why prodigals are, on occasion, the products of godly parents—just as I cannot explain how children who love the Lord sometimes come from homes that are woefully weak spiritually. This reality makes us all the more dependent on the Lord for His grace and power to work in the lives of our children. ...

If you are a parent, let me simply encourage you to do all in your power to battle the wrong and cultivate the right. Do all you can to point your children in the direction of Jesus Christ. Let all your love and your faith be evident to them. Walk your talk . . . and then leave the results to God.

CHARLES SWINDOLL,
THE LIVING INSIGHTS STUDY BIBLE[7]

12

Watching Them Soar

If I have nurtured, encouraged, directed and supported you, my children, then letting go should be a natural step. Trusting you to fly on your own is the best way I can show you my love.

YVONNE OHUMUKINI URNESS, IN *A MOTHER'S TOUCH*

Graduation is over!

She has taken a job with an internet start-up company far away from home.

He is going to graduate school and has assumed responsibility for his own financial aid.

He's joined the army.

You've planned the wedding, walked her down the aisle and waved goodbye.

He's traveling in Europe before settling down.

Finally, they are launched. Soaring. Flying free.

You feel proud ... sad ... lonely ... exhilarated ... frightened about your own future ... ambivalent ... empty ... all mixed up.

We raise our children to leave us. Why, then, does it feel like this when they go? Why is the empty house suddenly so empty and the silence so loud?

Parents face a period of adjustment in this season of life, a time often filled with conflicting confusing emotions. We have to remember that letting go is a process with dual purposes: it weans a child from the parents and weans parents from the child. Yet the weaning process often involves some pain. And then there's that word *empty* in empty nest. It sounds so pathetic. So empty. As if life is devoid of content when the kids leave home.

We feel a real loss. In fact, we may experience the stages of grief common to those mourning a death. Mourning is a normal reaction to any loss, whether it be death, divorce, or another kind of separation, such as children leaving home. James Lynch says,

> The ultimate price exacted for commitment to other human beings rests in the inescapable fact that loss and pain will be experienced when they are gone.... Like the rise and fall of the ocean tides, disruptions of human relationships occur at regular intervals throughout life, and include ... children leaving home.[1]

GRIEVING THE LOSS

Hospice, a national organization that helps families deal with death and dying, offers support to people in bereavement. They gently assure a grieving person that his or her feelings are normal and healthy and that the expression of those feelings gets a person through the grieving process more quickly and comfortably.

"We allowed ourselves to grieve when our final child left the nest," one mother confided to me. "We experienced a sense of deep loss and all the pain that goes with it, but I know we've come through it more prepared for God's next challenge because of our grieving process."

> *We need to acknowledge our feelings about the separation.*
> ∽✕∽

In other words, we need to acknowledge our feelings about the separation. We may feel depressed, confused, listless, and unmotivated. These feelings are real but temporary. There will be brighter moments, even rewards, ahead.

Grieving is a period of transition. As I said in my book *A Mother's Footprints of Faith,*

Life is filled with transitions; bridges between what was and what will be. Sometimes those bridges seem wobbly, insecure, or risky, because we have to leave where we've been in order to reach the place where we are going. We have to let go of the past before we can fully embrace the future.

We don't stay on these bridges of transition; they are temporary, in-between places of growing and becoming. However, we don't notice our growth until we reach the other side and look back. Only then do we realize that God has put those bridges in our path, and has walked with us across the span of uncertain territory to security on the the other side.[2]

HARDER FOR MOTHERS OR FOR FATHERS?

Is the empty nest adjustment more difficult for a mother or for a father? It's risky to stereotype the responses. The adjustment may be more painful for the mother if she has stayed home to care for her family through the years, especially if this was the main source of her identity. She may find herself with "nothing to do" and little self-confidence to seek a change. However, few women reach the empty nest season totally unprepared for fulfillment beyond motherhood. Because of our increased life span, women enter this season with an awareness of the opportunities and options available to us in this period of increased freedom.

Many fathers feel more empty nest grief than previously thought, though they may have more trouble talking about it. Some fathers say they feel older and are nostalgic about the loss of chances to make memories with their children. They regret the busyness of their lives that robbed them of opportunities to spend more time with their children.

One father said God had the time frame mixed up. His job required his maximum time and energy when his kids were young and needed him most. Nearly twenty years later when his job-related pressures and responsibilities slackened, his children were leaving home.

OTHER FACTORS

The empty nest season may coincide with other life-altering experiences. For women, it may be menopause. For both men and women, it may be a midlife crisis, that time when one confronts the passage of time and reexamines life-governing values and priorities. It may trigger a move to a smaller house or motivate a remodeling job, turning children's former bedrooms into offices, guest rooms, or even a duplex rental unit. All these changes can cause stress.

The empty nest may also coincide with the death or impending death of our parents. "I feel tugged by both generations," explained one mother. "My son is packing up to go off to college, and my father is dying of cancer. I'm facing a double loss; I feel confused and even angry."

As our parents get older, we examine our relationship with them and in turn our relationship with our children. "Although I'm sure he loved me, my father never showed much affection," one father lamented. "Now that my son is ready to leave home, I'm afraid I haven't hugged him or told him I love him often enough."

In dealing with older parents, we often face a role reversal that takes an emotional toll. Instead of them taking care of us, we begin to take care of them in subtle little ways. We drive the car instead of letting them drive. We remind them to take a sweater in case it gets chilly. We help them decide what to order from the menu and even cut their meat. If this role reversal coincides with the emptying of the nest, we feel a keener awareness of the passing of time. Our children's leaving and the changes in our parents both remind us of our mortality.

The marriage relationship usually undergoes a change during the empty nest season. Suddenly, we set only two places at the table and have more time to think about this person who shares the salad.

"When children leave there is more time to notice and confront each other. The buffer and distraction of children is no longer present. Often the romance and passion of the earlier years are gone, the adhesive that is very much needed but is so difficult to generate once again," writes H. Norman Wright in *Seasons of a Marriage*.[3]

For all these reasons and more, the empty nest years can be a daunting challenge that is downright painful to walk through. Some days we may feel weak as we face the transition. But as James Russell Lowell wrote:

> There are two kinds of weakness: that which
> breaks and that which bends.[4]

In her book *A Time to Grieve*, Carol Staudacher comments on Lowell's lines, "What we may consider to be weakness can actually be strength. . . . We lean, we bend, we rearrange, we figure out another approach, we soften—but we don't break."[5]

GET ON WITH IT!

We can turn the empty nest challenge into an opportunity.

"I moped around the house for two weeks after our youngest left for college, but I didn't cry," one mother told me. "On Friday afternoon of the second week, I was wheeling the shopping cart through the grocery store and stopped in the cereal section. Suddenly it hit me. I didn't need to buy Wheat Chex anymore, and the tears came. I stood there crying for a long time. But then I came home to a clean house with no dirty laundry, and my husband and I had a great weekend of freedom alone together. And I liked it!"

Sometimes God shakes us up to motivate us to grow and change. Many parents on the other side of the empty nest adjustment give glowing reports of their new lives. One husband said, "When our last child left home, it was ecstasy!"

This is the time to honestly confront the challenge of deciding what to do with the rest of your life. One mother wrote these words after her daughter left for college:

> *This is the time to honestly confront the challenge of deciding what to do with the rest of our lives.*

Yes, a dangerous time. It involves a break with the past, the anticipation of a sudden freedom, no kids in the house, a new beginning for the mother, as if she too and not only the daughter were taking off into her own life. Anything possible. Future unknown. Time for the unlived life to rise up and stake its claim. Everything you might have been but didn't become; anything you might have wished to be but put aside. Now's your chance.[6]

Author and speaker Jill Briscoe enthusiastically told a group of women at a seminar, "This is a marvelous time of life! You want to go back to work? Super! The working world needs vibrant Christian women being light in dark places."

Many women are discovering their fifties to be the best years of their lives. That's encouraging information that needs to be passed down to younger moms who, like me, dreaded the dismal sound of "empty nest."

> *Many women are discovering their fifties to be the best years of their lives.*
>
>

As with many major changes in our lives, we can choose our attitude. We can dwell on the negative or focus on the positive. Finally I can trade the minivan in on a sportier car! Finally we have leftovers in the house again. Finally the public service bill is down and so is the volume on the stereo; even the choice of music is ours alone. We can be impulsive: make dinner or choose not to make dinner, or go away for a weekend on a moment's notice. The bathroom is clean, and the evenings give us stretches of time for ourselves.

Carolyn Johnson comments on life for her and her husband after the children left home:

> Harry and I together have dabbled in the study of subjects from genealogy to desert creepy crawlies. We've explored the United States by motorhome and walked in the footsteps of Jesus in Israel. At home, we have hobbies we pursue separately that make our time together more interesting.
>
> The point is, in order to keep from leaning too heavily on our adult children, we have found interests and activities outside our parenthood roles—new horizons. We may be limited in our choices by the state of our budget or health, but there is an opportunity or a need in our community to fit each of us.[7]

If you are not yet able to see the empty nest challenge as an opportunity, take your grief and fear and future to God and pray for his peace and guidance in this next season of your life. What good purpose does he have for you? Pray in faith, believing in his lovingkindness. He wants the best for you more than you want the best for your children.

PRAY FOR YOUR CHILDREN

Anytime, anywhere, at any age, we can pray for our children. Sometimes, after they're gone and are living hundreds of miles away, it feels as if that's about all we can do for them. In the last paragraph of her book about being the parents of adult children, Carolyn Johnson says, "As parents of adults who are beyond our authority, our part is to pray that they will find peace in recognizing the authority of God."[8]

Now that my children have grown and gone, I pray for them each morning, adapting the prayer that Jesus, shortly before his death, prayed for his disciples (John 17:6–26). In my own paraphrase, I pray that:

- They will be protected from the evil one, both physically and spiritually. Physically in their safety as they go from place to place. Spiritually so that God's truth protects them from anything that is not from him, such as discouragement or fear or lack of confidence.

- They will seek his will, know his will, and make choices according to his will, and that those choices will shape and grow them and conform them to his image.

- They will have a godly person to walk alongside them and hold up their arms when they grow weary and point them back to Jesus if they get off the track.

Praying for our children will always remain part of our job description, even when our active parenting responsibilities are over.

REWARDS

The late Erma Bombeck, known for her wit and sensitivity as a wife and mother, compared raising a child to flying a kite. She said we spend a lifetime trying to get them off the ground, running with them, trying again and again.

Finally they are airborne: they need more string and you keep letting it out. But with each twist of the ball of twine, there is a sadness that goes with joy. The kite becomes more distant, and you know it won't be long before that beautiful creature will snap the lifeline that binds you together and will soar as it is meant to soar, free and alone. Only then do you know that you did your job.[9]

The blessings of release will be greater than we ever imagined. Remember the story of Hannah, who was barren for so many years. She finally had a son, Samuel, and gave him to the Lord. In return she was richly blessed with five more children. And Samuel grew to serve God mightily. What better reward could a mother receive?

The blessings come in different packages. One mother, Joan Mills, writes that she discovered the best part of parenting when her grown children left home. "The generations smile at one another, as if exchanging congratulations. The children are no longer children. The parents are awed to discover adults," and that, she concludes, "is the final, firmest bonding; the goal and the reward."[10]

When our children grow up and leave home, our active parenting responsibilities are over. We have trained them, loved them dearly, and stirred up the nest to release them. We will always love them, always pray for them, but our work is done. Yet God promises us that the end is always a beginning. This is the end of one season but the beginning of a new one with a new opportunity to start a new adventure with the Lord.

It is a time to soar freely.

> Those who hope in the LORD will renew their
>   strength.
> They will soar on wings like eagles;
> they will run and not grow weary,
> they will walk and not be faint.
>
> *Isaiah 40:31*

FOR REFLECTION

1. What are some of the rewards of the empty nest season of life? Drawbacks?

2. As you face or look forward to the empty nest years, what plans do you have?

3. What might keep you from realizing these plans?

4. If you are living in an empty nest, describe the grieving process you experienced.

5. Write a prayer for each of your children, taking into consideration his or her unique bent and life circumstances. Regarding each child, what do you thank God for? If you were to ask your child to pray for you in this season of life, what would that prayer be?

PONDERPOINT

WHAT A MOTHER SAYS

Oh, let me hold her!
How's my little angel?
Hush, baby girl.
Aren't you sleepy yet?
It's okay. Don't cry.
No, no. Don't touch.
Come to Mommy.
Take that out of your mouth. Yucky!
That's not for you.
You don't need that anymore.
You're a big girl now.
Tell Mommy if you need to go potty . . . okay?

Don't get into your brother's things.
Go to your room.
No, you may not.
I just brought a drink of water.
Get back in bed.
Pick up your toys.
Don't play inside the clothes rack.
Can you draw a picture for Grandma?
Hold still.
Can you remember to bring it home tomorrow?
I'm sure she still wants to be your friend.
Did you practice?
Try looking under your bed.
Go wash your hands.
You're not old enough yet.
You'll have to ask your father.
Where was it when you last saw it?
Stop teasing your brother.
Go clean your room. Come set the table.
Don't bite your nails.
Did you do your homework?
Get off the phone. Eat your vegetables.
You're responsible to keep track of your own
    things.
Did you tell me it was this Saturday?
Sure—if you want to use your own money.
Tell her you'll call her back.
Try on a bigger size.
There's a boy on the phone for you.
You may not wear that to school.
Be back by your curfew.
I did not say it was okay.
Come straight home.

No, I need the car this afternoon.

Are you coming home this weekend? Next
  weekend?

What do you know about him?

Have you thought this through?

I ordered them because I thought you'd appreciate
  them.

But pink used to be your favorite color.

Whatever you want. It's up to you.

Don't sit on your veil.

Call us when you get there. Don't slip on the rice.

Good-bye, honey.

ROBIN JONES GUNN, *MOTHERING BY HEART*[11]

Epilogue

My baby is getting married.

A few weeks after I write this, twenty-three-year-old Kendall will put on a beautiful long white gown, take the arm of her father, and walk down an aisle to take the hand of a handsome young man named David. Then, before God and a church of family and friends, she will vow her lifelong commitment to a whole new priority of love and relationships. She will emerge with a new name and a new home halfway across the country from where she grew up.

I'm sure I will cry. Mostly for joy, because this wedding and this young man are the answers to our prayers that Kendall would marry someone who loves God and cherishes her. But I'll also have this tiny sad spot in my heart that wonders how Kendall's marriage will change our close relationship. It's a question that has been poking at me during the last several months of hectic wedding preparations.

Because Kendall is the first of my two daughters to get married, this mother-of-the-bride role is new for me. I was mother of the groom two years ago and tried to carry out the traditional job description of "wearing beige and keeping my mouth shut."

But Kendall is my *baby,* and this time, the job description feels more complicated. I knew I'd need some help, and so, shortly after her engagement, I sought the advice of friends who had been through this experience.

"Let the bride and groom make all the important decisions," one friend warned. "In fact, it's probably best if you simply have no opinion."

I heeded her advice and did just fine with cake flavors and flower colors and musical selections and the style of bridesmaids' dresses. But I surprised myself with the passion I felt about the lighting of the unity candle which is a traditional part of the wedding ceremony, symbolizing the couple's two lives becoming one. Usually, after the guests are seated, the two mothers come forward and light two candles representing the bride and the groom. Then, following the exchange of wedding vows and rings, the bride and groom take the candles and together light the single unity candle. Now here's the choice: do they blow out their individual candles or leave them burning? It can be done either way, but when the discussion came up, I suddenly couldn't stand the thought of Kendall blowing her candle out.

"Don't," I begged in a vulnerable moment late one evening. Kendall and I were sitting on stools pulled up to the kitchen counter, her wedding planner spread out before us. Lynn had long since turned in, growing increasingly less interested in these details.

Kendall looked at me, confused by the emotion in my voice. "I'll talk to David," she mumbled, an increasingly familiar (and appropriate) response.

Obviously she didn't understand what I only now understand about my reaction that night, a reaction that doesn't have much to do with candles and flames. It's about loving and letting go. This is what I meant to say: "The flame of your candle represents who you are as an individual and all you bring of yourself to this union. It represents the family you grew up in and all the love poured into helping shape you into the person you are today."

Even now as I think about these words, I hear my passion crescendoing as I deliver my final plea: "Don't blow your candle out, Kendall! That's like snuffing us out of your life."

Granted this message sounds a bit melodramatic, but as the mother of the bride, surely I get the privilege of being emotional at a time like this. The fact is, I still don't know whether Kendall will blow her candle out. (I'm tempted to substitute one of those trick candles that re-ignites when you try to blow it out, just in case she tries.)

Yet not knowing how the candle saga will turn out seems somehow fitting as I finish this book, because I see this as another of God's gentle reminders that letting go is a lifelong challenge marked by constant changes in relationships and circumstances. And when it comes to our children, especially as they grow up and leave home, we have to trust that when we let go of the way things are, we are making room for the way God intends them to become. We have to trust him in the face of the unknowns.

With this faith, each letting go marks a new beginning filled with hope.

So I intend to face this challenge of letting go in the same way I've faced all the rest, with a prayer of surrender, which will fill me with hope as we celebrate a new beginning in our family.

Dear Heavenly Father,

Today, as I help plan my daughter's wedding, I lift her—my child whom I've loved and nurtured for twenty-three years—up to you with a prayer of surrender.

Though she will be less of my child, I know she will always be your child.

Though she will be moving farther away from me, I pray she will be moving closer to you.

Protect her, please, Lord. Seal in her heart any eternal truths she has learned up 'til now. And keep her heart tender and open to those still ahead.

Bless her marriage. Thank you for the love she and David have for each other and for you. And may that love always surround them and help them continue to grow into the people you've created them to be.

As for the tiny little sad place in my heart ... I carry it today as a reminder that loving our children the way you call us to love them always has a cost. So this is a sweet sadness. Still, I surrender it to you, knowing that you will make it grow smaller and smaller until it disappears in the hope of this new beginning in our family. Amen.

Notes

CHAPTER 1: STIRRING UP THE NEST

1. Ron Hutchcraft, *Five Needs Your Child Must Have Met at Home* (Grand Rapids: Zondervan, 1994), 141.
2. Donald Joy, *Bonding* (Waco: Word, 1985), 123–24.

CHAPTER 2: HEAD KNOWLEDGE AND HEART FEELINGS

1. James C. Dobson, "Setting Your Adolescent Free" (Arcadia, Calif.: Focus on the Family), abstracted from James C. Dobson, *The Strong-Willed Child* (Wheaton, Ill.: Tyndale House, 1978).
2. Nancy P. McConnell, "Thoughts on Motherhood" (Colorado Springs: Current, Inc., 1983).
3. "'Parent Burnout': Latest Sign of Today's Stresses," interview with Joseph Procaccini in *U.S. News and World Report* (7 March 1983), 76–77.
4. Anonymous, "Our Teenage Daughter Ran Away," *Good Housekeeping* (January 1984), 28–34.
5. Tim Brennan, Delbert S. Elliott, and David Huizinga, *The Social Psychology of Runaways* (Lexington, Mass.: D.C. Heath and Co., Lexington Books, 1978), 160.
6. Kevin Leman, *Parenthood without Hassles—Well, Almost* (Irvine, Calif.: Harvest House), as quoted in "Dear Abby," *Daily Camera* (13 January 1981).
7. Dolores Curran, *Traits of a Healthy Family* (Minneapolis: Winston Press, 1983), 166, 184.
8. Henry Cloud and John Townsend, *Boundaries for Kids* (Grand Rapids: Zondervan: 1998), 67–68.
9. Elizabeth Cody Newenhuyse, *Sometimes I Feel Like Running Away from Home* (Minneapolis: Bethany House, 1993), 46–47.
10. Quoted in John Trent, Ph.D., with Erin M. Healy, *My Mother's Hands* (Colorado Springs: Waterbrook Press, 2000), 101.

CHAPTER 3: CONTROL AND SURRENDER

1. Margie M. Lewis, "Hope for the Hurting Parent" (Arcadia, Calif: Focus on the Family, 1983), booklet excerpted from *The Hurting Parent* (Grand Rapids: Zondervan, 1980).
2. Harriet Lerner, *Mother Dance* (New York: Harper Perennial, 1999), 7.
3. Gien Karssen, *Her Name Is Woman, Book 1* (Downers Grove, Ill.: InterVarsity, 1975), 88.
4. A. W. Tozer, *The Pursuit of God*, special ed. (Wheaton, Ill.; Tyndale, n.d.), 26.

CHAPTER 4: OVERCOMING MOMMY FEARS

1. Judith Viorst, *Necessary Losses* (New York: Simon and Schuster, 1986), 206.
2. Karen Scalf Linamen, *Happily Ever After* (Grand Rapids: Revell, 1997), 186.
3. Henry Fairlie, "Fear of Living," *New Republic* (23 January 1989), 14.
4. Harriet Lerner, *Mother Dance* (New York: Harper Perennial, 1999), 7.
5. Dietrich Bonhoeffer, *Letters and Papers from Prison,* ed. Eberhard Bethge (New York: Macmillan, 1967), 117.
6. Miriam Huffman Rockness, *Home, God's Design* (Grand Rapids: Zondervan, 1990), 234–35.
7. Evelyn Bence, *Prayers for Girlfriends and Sisters and Me* (Ann Arbor: Servant, 1999), 90.

CHAPTER 5: PARENTAL PATTERNS

1. P. Roger Hillerstrom, *Your Family Voyage* (Grand Rapids: Revell, 1993), 31.
2. Hillerstrom, *Your Family Voyage,* 162.
3. Harriet Lerner, *Mother Dance* (New York: HarperCollins, 1998), 291.
4. Quoted in Judith Viorst, *Imperfect Control* (New York: Simon and Schuster, 1998), 164.
5. Viorst, *Imperfect Control,* 164.
6. Quoted in Viorst, *Imperfect Control,* 164.
7. Catherine Marshall, *To Live Again* (Charlotte: Commission Press, 1957), 119.
8. Phyllis Theroux, "What Your Kids Really Want," *American Home* (May 1977), 37.
9. David Elkind, *The Hurried Child* (Reading, Mass.: Addison-Wesley, 1981), 30.

10. Evelyn Bence, *Leaving Home* (Wheaton, Ill.: Tyndale House, 1986), 137–38.

11. Erma Bombeck, *Motherhood, The Second Oldest Profession* (New York: McGraw-Hill, 1983), 30.

12. Michael V. Bloom, *Adolescent-Parental Separation* (New York: Gardner Press, 1980), 53.

13. Henry Cloud and John Townsend, *The Mom Factor* (Grand Rapids: Zondervan, 1996), 227.

CHAPTER 6: BUILDING A FIRM FOUNDATION

1. Karen Scalf Linamen, "Family with a Purpose," *Today's Christian Woman* (July-August 1998), 56.

2. Judy Downs Douglass, *What Can a Mother Do?* (San Bernardino, Calif.: Here's Life, 1988), citing Kay and Jan Kuzma, *Building Character* (Mt. View, Calif.: Pacific Press, 1979).

3. Larry Christenson, *The Christian Family* (Minneapolis: Bethany House, 1970), 165.

4. Christenson, *The Christian Family*, 65.

5. Hughes Mearns, "Every Child Has a Gift," *Keys to Happiness* (Pleasantville, N.Y.: Reader's Digest Association, 1955), 223–26.

6. Phyllis Theroux, "What Your Kids Really Want," *American Home* (May 1977), 37.

7. Janet Chester Bly, *If My Kids Drive Me Crazy, Am I a Bad Mom?* (Colorado Springs: NavPress, 1991), 18.

CHAPTER 7: EARLY TRAINING RULES

1. Elisa Morgan and Carol Kuykendall, *What Every Child Needs* (Grand Rapids: Zondervan, 1997), 18–19.

2. Henry Cloud and John Townsend, *Raising Great Kids* (Grand Rapids: Zondervan, 1999), 71.

3. Ibid., 124.

4. Henry Cloud and John Townsend, *Boundaries* (Grand Rapids: Zondervan, 1992), 66.

5. Bernice Weissbourd, "Declarations of Dependence," *Parents* (January 1983), 70.

6. Mary White, *Developing Your Child's Devotional Life* (Arcadia, Calif.: Focus on the Family, 1982), booklet excerpted from Mary White, *Successful Family Devotions* (Colorado Springs: Navigators Press, 1981).

7. Adapted from Elisa Morgan and Carol Kuykendall, *What Every Child Needs* (Grand Rapids: Zondervan, 1997).

CHAPTER 8: THE MIDDLE YEARS

1. Bob Barnes, *Ready for Responsibility* (Grand Rapids: Zondervan, 1997), 40.
2. Henry Cloud and John Townsend, *Boundaries with Kids* (Grand Rapids: Zondervan, 1998), 15.
3. Nan K. Chase, "Teaching Your Children Independence Skills," *Washington Post* (15 February 2000), C–4.
4. Elisa Morgan and Carol Kuykendall, *What Every Child Needs* (Grand Rapids: Zondervan, 1997), 54.
5. Nancy Lloyd, "Raising Money-Wise Children," *Washington Post* (2 March 2000), C–4.
6. Cloud and Townsend, *Raising Great Kids,* 174–75.
7. Bob Barnes, *Ready for Responsibility* (Grand Rapids: Zondervan, 1997), 202.
8. Quoted in John Trent with Erin M. Healy, *My Mother's Hands* (Colorado Springs: Waterbrook, 2000), 97.

CHAPTER 9: ADOLESCENCE

1. Michael V. Bloom, *Adolescent-Parental Separation* (New York: Gardner Press, 1980), 42.
2. Jay Kesler, *Too Big to Spank* (Ventura, Calif.: Regal Books, 1978), 89.
3. Henry Cloud and John Townsend, *Raising Great Kids* (Grand Rapids: Zondervan, 1999), 187.
4. Tim Brennan, Delbert S. Elliott, and David Huizinga, *The Social Psychology of Runaways* (Lexington, Mass.: D.C. Heath and Co., Lexington Books, 1978), 156–58.
5. Haim G. Ginott, *Between Parent and Teenager* (New York: Macmillan, 1969), 111.
6. Carol Kuykendall, *Give Them Wings* (Colorado Springs: Focus on the Family, 1994), 124.
7. Interview with Delbert S. Elliott, behavioral researcher.
8. "The Christian Family," *New Life Magazine* (January 1983), 7.
9. Kuyekndall, *Give Them Wings,* 22.
10. John White, *Parents in Pain* (Downers Grove, Ill.: InterVarsity, 1979) 164–65.

CHAPTER 10: FACING TRANSITIONS: "GET A LIFE, MOM!"

1. H. Norman Wright, *Seasons of a Marriage* (Ventura Calif.: Regal Books, 1982), 90.

2. Marguerite Beecher and Willard Beecher, *Parents on the Run?* as quoted in *Dr. Dobson Answers Your Questions* (Wheaton, Ill.: Tyndale, 1982), 206.

3. Henry Cloud and John Townsend, *Boundaries* (Grand Rapids, Zondervan, 1992), 29.

4. Anne Morrow Lindbergh, *Gift from the Sea* (New York: Pantheon, 1955), introduction.

5. Elisa Morgan and Carol Kuykendall, *What Every Mom Needs* (Grand Rapids: Zondervan, 1995), 68.

CHAPTER 11: FUZZY RELEASE

1. Michael V. Bloom, *Adolescent-Parental Separation* (New York: Gardner Press, 1980), 73.

2. Robert Frost, "The Death of the Hired Man," *Robert Frost's Poems* (New York: Pocket Books, 1971), 165.

3. Focus on the Family Reader's Poll, Arcadia, California, 1981.

4. Evelyn Bence, *Leaving Home* (Wheaton, Ill.: Tyndale, 1986), 142.

5. Paul Tournier, *The Meaning of Gifts* (Atlanta: John Knox Press, 1963), 28.

6. Elinor Lenz, *Once My Child, Now My Friend* (New York: Warner Books, 1981), 7.

7. Charles Swindoll, *The Living Insights Study Bible* (Grand Rapids: Zondervan, 1996), 368.

CHAPTER 12: WATCHING THEM SOAR

1. James J. Lynch, *The Broken Heart*, quoted in Ray Ashford, *The Surrender and the Singing: Happiness through Letting Go* (Minneapolis: Winston Press, 1985), 84–85.

2. Carol Kuykendall, *A Mother's Footprints of Faith* (Grand Rapids: Zondervan, 1997), 49.

3. H. Norman Wright, *Seasons of a Marriage* (Ventura, Calif.: Regal Books, 1982), 55.

4. James Russell Lowell, quoted in Carol Staudacher, *A Time to Grieve* (San Francisco: HarperSanFrancisco, 1994), 144.

5. Staudacher, *A Time to Grieve,* 144.

6. Harriet Lerner, *Mother Dance* (New York: HarperCollins, 1998), 295.

7. Carolyn Johnson, *Forever a Parent: Relating to Your Adult Children* (Grand Rapids: Zondervan, 1992), 161.

8. Johnson, *Forever a Parent,* 173.

9. Erma Bombeck, "At Wit's End," Field Newspaper Syndicate (2 May 1978).

10. Joan Mills, "When My Grown Children Left Home," in *Focus on the Family* (November 1983), reprinted from *Reader's Digest* (January 1981).

11. Robin Jones Gunn, *Mothering by Heart* (Sisters, Oreg.: Questar Publishers, 1996), 69–70. Used by permission.

The MOPS Story

MOPS stands for Mothers of Preschoolers, a program designed to encourage mothers with children under school age through relationships and resources. These women come from different backgrounds and lifestyles, yet have similar needs and a shared desire to be the best mothers they can be!

A MOPS group provides a caring, accepting atmosphere for today's mother of preschoolers. Here she has an opportunity to share concerns, explore areas of creativity, and hear instruction that equips her for the responsibilities of family and community. The MOPS group also includes MOPPETS, a loving, learning experience for children.

Approximately 2,500 groups meet in churches throughout the United States, Canada, and 13 other countries, to meet the needs of more than 100,000 women. Many more mothers are encouraged by MOPS resources, including MOMSense radio and magazine, MOPS' web site, and publications such as this book.

Find out how MOPS International can help you become part of the MOPS♥to♥Mom Connection.

MOPS International
P.O. Box 102200
Denver, CO 80250-2200
Phone 1-800-929-1287 or 303-733-5353
E-mail: Info@MOPS.org
Web site: http://www.MOPS.org

To learn how to start a MOPS group,
call 1-888-910-MOPS.
For MOPS products call The MOPShop
1-888-545-4040.

We want to hear from you. Please send your comments about this
book to us in care of the address below. Thank you.

ZondervanPublishingHouse

Grand Rapids, Michigan 49530

http://www.zondervan.com